Reaching Out

Reaching Out
making a difference in your world

For a free catalog
of NavPress books & Bible studies call
1-800-366-7788 (USA) or 1-800-839-4769 (Canada).
www.NavPress.com

The Navigators is an international Christian organization. Our mission is to advance the gospel of Jesus and His kingdom into the nations through spiritual generations of laborers living and discipling among the lost. We see a vital movement of the gospel, fueled by prevailing prayer, flowing freely through relational networks and out into the nations where workers for the kingdom are next door to everywhere.

NavPress is the publishing ministry of The Navigators. The mission of NavPress is to reach, disciple, and equip people to know Christ and make Him known by publishing life-related materials that are biblically rooted and culturally relevant. Our vision is to stimulate spiritual transformation through every product we publish.

© 2008 Youth for Christ International Ministries
All rights reserved. No part of this publication may be reproduced in any form without written permission from NavPress, P.O. Box 35001, Colorado Springs, CO 80935. www.navpress.com

NAVPRESS and the NAVPRESS logo are registered trademarks of NavPress. Absence of ® in connection with marks of NavPress or other parties does not indicate an absence of registration of those marks.

ISBN-13: 978-1-60006-313-8
ISBN-10: 1-60006-313-6

Cover design by Arvid Wallen
Cover image by Shutterstock

Some of the anecdotal illustrations in this book are true to life and are included with the permission of the persons involved. All other illustrations are composites of real situations, and any resemblance to people living or dead is coincidental.

Unless otherwise identified, all Scripture quotations in this publication are taken from the *Holy Bible, New Living Translation* (NLT), copyright © 1996, 2004. Used by permission of Tyndale House Publishers, Inc., Carol Stream, Illinois 60188. All rights reserved.

Printed in the United States of America

1 2 3 4 5 6 7 8 / 12 11 10 09 08

Contents

Acknowledgments	7
Introduction	9
SESSION ONE: Reasons to Share	13
SESSION TWO: God's Story and My Story	21
SESSION THREE: My Story and Your Story	27
SESSION FOUR: God's Story and Your Story	33
SESSION FIVE: Friendship Evangelism	39
SESSION SIX: Prayer Evangelism	45
SESSION SEVEN: Prayer Groups	49
SESSION EIGHT: Power Evangelism	55
SESSION NINE: Who We Are in God's Eyes	59
SESSION TEN: Meeting the Needs of Others	65
SESSION ELEVEN: Being a Servant Leader (PART 1)	73
SESSION TWELVE: Being a Servant Leader (PART 2)	81

Bonus!
Be Bold!	93
What it Means to Believe in Jesus	99
Evangelism Is Important	101
Go and Do the Same	103
Hope for a Nation	105

Small Group Leader's Guide
How to Lead a Small Group	111
Group Discussion Starters	113
Youth for Christ	121

Acknowledgments

We are indebted to the many dedicated men and women of Youth for Christ over numerous years who have worked tirelessly to bring this material to you in its current form. In this regard, we are grateful to the following people:

Lori Hill	Emmanuel Kingi
Joy Englesman	Ken Aringo
Don Osman	Nthenya Masyuko
Dave Bidwell	Lucy Miruka
Emmanuel Chijindu	Lawrence Odhiambo
Cyprian Yobera	Beatrice Wangwe
Seneiya Kamotho	Felix Mwangi
Nick Sikobe	Gowi Odera
Sandy Weiss	T.V.O. Lamptey
Banda Banda-di-Mamoso	Jane Gumo
Ayo Ipinmoye	Jack and Polly Wilson
George Tabu Jabulani	Chris Harding

We are also indebted to our brothers and sisters from all over Africa who birthed this project and field-tested it as part of the Generation 21 initiative. Through the vision God gave them of empowering young leaders for their continent, this material was developed.

As the worldwide movement of Youth for Christ has adopted this same focus of empowering young leaders, we have modified and adapted this material for worldwide use.

Reaching Out

This material is used as a tool to achieve Youth for Christ's strategic focus of reaching young people everywhere, working together with the local church and other like-minded partners to raise up lifelong followers of Jesus who lead by their godliness in lifestyle, devotion to the Word of God and prayer, passion for sharing the love of Christ, and commitment to social involvement.

Introduction

>> "O Sovereign LORD," I said, "I can't speak for you! I'm too young!" The LORD replied, "Don't say, 'I'm too young,' for you must go wherever I send you and say whatever I tell you." (Jeremiah 1:6-7)

Perhaps you've felt like Jeremiah as he expressed his anxiety to God. There's a message to be shared, but you might feel too young, too inexperienced, too shy . . . or you might have another reason from a list of many why *you* shouldn't be the one to spread the message of God's love for the world. You may not "feel" like someone who should be charged with this responsibility, and you may not "feel" like you're supposed to be a leader. But this book will help you see that everyone who follows God is asked to share that message of His love and to serve others—whether we feel like it or not.

Yes, some people seem to have all the words and know exactly what to say when they talk about their relationship with God. Maybe when you see someone preaching, teaching, or sharing about his or her faith you think that person simply has a special gift from the Lord that you don't have. And while there are those who have evangelism skills, it's still something that God wants all of us to do because of our love for Him and those who don't yet know Him.

Many new followers of Jesus think that evangelism, or sharing the message of God's love and gift of salvation, is a special duty reserved for those who have been following Jesus for years. More often than not, we find ourselves thinking that we need experience or years of training to be effective at this.

However, the most important qualification for telling others about Jesus is that we know Him ourselves and we are His followers and friends. Once we know Jesus, it can be as simple as talking about a good friend we want someone else to know. Because we know Jesus and what He's done in our lives, we want others to experience that as well.

Of course, if you don't already have a relationship with Jesus, that's the most important thing to consider! Before you talk to others about Him, He needs to be your Lord. If you have not committed yourself to following Jesus, consider the verses that opened this section, and what they mean to your life. If you want to give your life to Jesus, you can pray to Him, ask Him to forgive your sins, and begin that relationship right now.

Here's an example of such a prayer:

Our Father in heaven, I know I haven't believed or had faith in you before, but I need your forgiveness and your peace. I believe that your Son, Jesus, died on a cross to pay the penalty for my faithlessness and showed His power over sin when He came back to life. I am so grateful that, because of this, I can be saved from an eternity of being separated from you. I want to serve you, Jesus, and to join my story with your story forever. I ask you to come into my life, to direct and take charge of me forever.

In Jesus' name I pray, amen.

The Bible says in Matthew 10:32, "Everyone who acknowledges me publicly here on earth, I will also acknowledge before my Father in heaven." So as we tell others of our faith, Jesus will tell His Father about us.

Now, if you have made a commitment to follow Jesus and obey Him, you want to be ready to share His message to others. If we are open and available to Jesus, He can use us to help our friends and family know Jesus also. We don't need a lot of experience, and we don't need to be great speakers or debaters; we just need to be open to sharing our experiences, listening to Jesus, and being available for Him to use us. Our greatest ability is our availability.

In this book you'll be challenged to share your faith, a process often called evangelism. Evangelism is simply a process of showing God's love to everyone by letting them know about Jesus. As a follower of Jesus, we are to love the people around us just like He does and want them to experience His great kindness to them. You'll learn more about how to do this and how to be a servant leader as you move through the sessions in this book.

Matthew 28:18-20 is one of the most well-known passages in Scripture that tells us to make followers, or disciples, of Jesus: "Jesus came and told his disciples, 'I have been given all authority in heaven and on earth. Therefore, go and make disciples of all the nations, baptizing them in the name of the Father and the Son and the Holy Spirit. Teach these new disciples to obey all the commands I have given you. And be sure of this: I am with you always, even to the end of the age.'"

Second Timothy 4:5 is another place in the Bible that reminds us of what God has called us to do: "But you should keep a clear mind in every situation. Don't be afraid of suffering for the Lord. Work at telling others the Good News, and fully carry out the ministry God has given you."

It's our privilege, as followers of Jesus, to be channels of God's love to the rest of the world so that they may get to know Jesus and have Him live in them. This is evangelism.

Evangelism means sharing the good news! The good news of Jesus Christ is such good news because we don't have to be good for it to be available to us. Good things are supposed to happen if you're good, but with Jesus, even when we are as bad as we think we could ever get, He still loves us. We can all receive His forgiveness and life forever if we believe and obey Him. The good news is that Jesus provides the entire solution to our problems of separation from God.

how to use this book

This book can be used with a group, or by a person wanting to move through this process alone. If you are doing this alone, simply read through each section, pausing to reflect on each question or comment you see. Write your thoughts here in this book, as you'll likely want to read them again at a later date to see how you've made progress as you learn to share your faith. You'll need only this book, a pen or pencil, and a Bible.

If you're doing this book with a group, you'll read through the sections aloud, and then pause to discuss the questions. Again, group members will want to write their thoughts and reflections to read again as they are growing in their abilities to share their faith. Each person will need a copy of this book, a pen or pencil, and a Bible.

If you're the one leading a small group through this book, you'll find additional helps later in the book. We've provided an optional discussion-starter or activity that will engage your group as you begin each session. Use these if you'd like. You'll also find additional helps on how to lead a group. See the Contents to find these additional sections in the book.

Over and over you'll find the same message in this book: We share our faith with others because of our love for them and our love for Jesus. May the love of Jesus fill your hearts and minds as you continue growing in your relationship with Him.

Reasons to Share

>> For everyone has sinned; we all fall short of God's glorious standard. (Romans 3:23)

For the wages of sin is death, but the free gift of God is eternal life through Christ Jesus our Lord. (Romans 6:23)

For God loved the world so much that he gave his one and only Son, so that everyone who believes in him will not perish but have eternal life. (John 3:16)

Let's start at the beginning and think about this: Why do we want to reach out in the first place? Good question! During this session we'll explore reasons to share our faith in Jesus with others.

reason 1: because we love our family and friends

All of us have people in our lives whom we love deeply, and we hope that we can be together with them forever. If these people also know and follow Jesus as their Lord and Savior, this hope will become a reality.

However, if these friends and family do *not* follow Jesus and accept Him

Reaching Out

as their Savior, they won't experience the joy of knowing Him and will be eternally separated from God, and from us, when they die.

Our love for our family and friends, and a longing for them to know Jesus and to be in a friendship with Him forever, is a strong motivation to share our faith with them.

Write the names of three people you know who you'd like to introduce to Jesus:

What do you think keeps these people you listed from being open to the love of Jesus? What could you say or do to help them see the truth?

> But how can they call on him to save them unless they believe in him? And how can they believe in him if they have never heard about him? And how can they hear about him unless someone tells them? (Romans 10:14)

How does this verse inspire you to tell others about Jesus?

reason 2: because we love God

You've probably heard people refer to "sharing the gospel." The "gospel" is Jesus—His story, His life, His death, and His resurrection. Jesus loved us enough to give up His own life for each of us. We show our love for God by believing in Him, following Him, and sharing that love with others.

In John 14:21 Jesus says, "Those who accept my commandments and obey them are the ones who love me. And because they love me, my Father will love them. And I will love them and reveal myself to each of them."

Do you think love and obedience go together? Why or why not? Why do you think Jesus links them together here?

In Matthew 28:19-20 Jesus gave His last commandment to His followers. He said, "Therefore, go and make disciples of all the nations, baptizing them in the name of the Father and the Son and the Holy Spirit. Teach these new disciples to obey all the commands I have given you. And be sure of this: I am with you always, even to the end of the age."

Based on this verse, what can you determine that Jesus wants you to do? If you accept the idea that love and obedience go together, how would your love for Jesus motivate you to obey this commandment of His?

reason 3: it's a privilege to share about Jesus

Did you know that the early followers of Jesus, many of whom were literally tortured or killed simply for following Jesus, considered it an honor to be able to tell others about Him? Check out a few of the verses where they express this themselves:

> By God's grace and mighty power, I have been given the privilege of serving him by spreading this Good News. Though I am the least

deserving of all God's people, he graciously gave me the privilege of telling the Gentiles about the endless treasures available to them in Christ. (Ephesians 3:7-8)

So we are Christ's ambassadors; God is making his appeal through us. We speak for Christ when we plead, "Come back to God!" (2 Corinthians 5:20)

We loved you so much that we shared with you not only God's Good News but our own lives, too. (1 Thessalonians 2:8)

What are activities you would normally consider a privilege to do?

Have you ever considered sharing about Jesus to be a privilege? How do these verses challenge to expand your thinking?

reasons why we don't share

No matter how much we love our family and friends, and no matter how much we love God and want to share His love with others, obstacles can get in the way. Here are a few you might be thinking of:

- My friends don't seem to be interested.
- My friends say they already believe in God.
- I don't know how to get the conversation started, or I don't know what to say.

- I'm embarrassed to talk about Jesus.
- I'm too busy.
- My own life is kind of messed up, so I don't think I'm a very good example of someone who should be talking about God.
- I might lose my friends if I talk to them about Jesus.
- I don't want people to laugh at me.

What are one or two other reasons you might not be excited about telling others about Jesus?

Okay, here's some good news! God has given us ways to get around those obstacles. Read these verses. Under each verse write a resource God provides or an idea or two that the verse suggests.

Matthew 10:20

Colossians 4:2-6

2 Timothy 3:16-17

Matthew 18:19-20

Colossians 3:12-15

Reaching Out

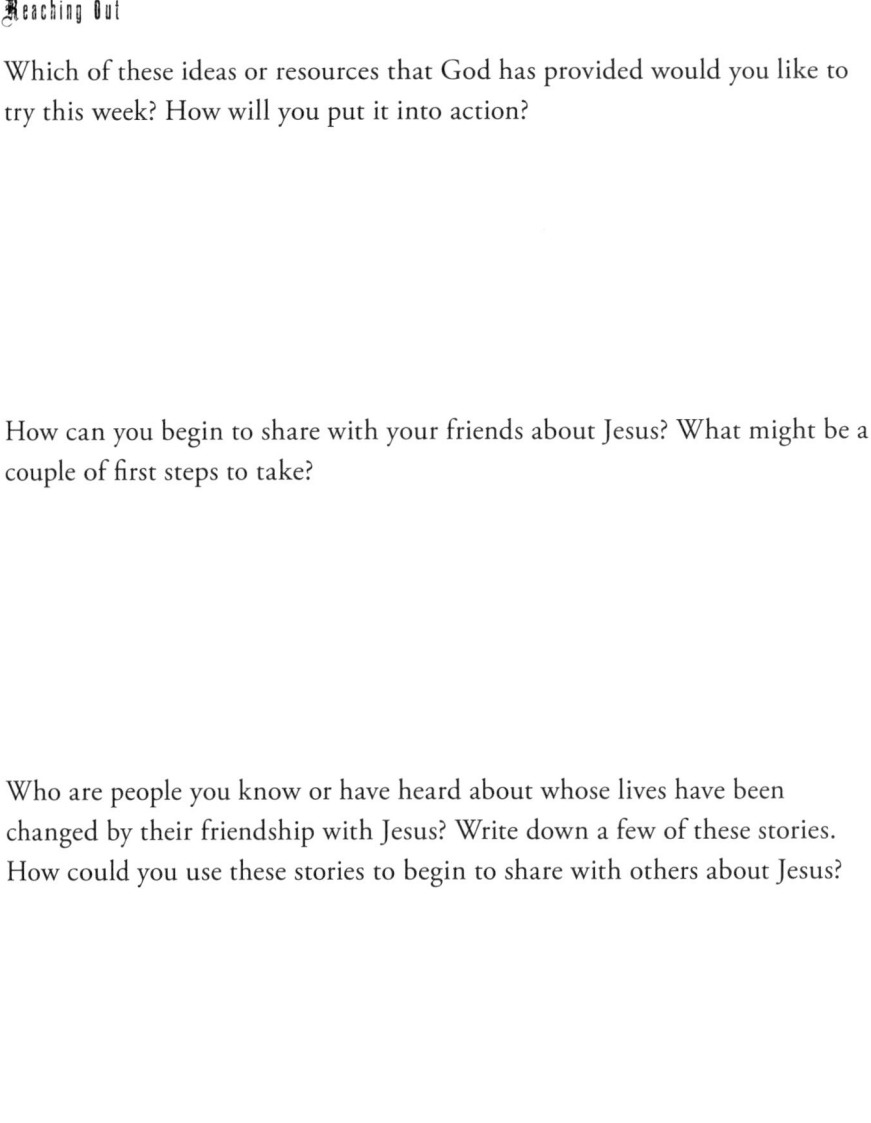

Which of these ideas or resources that God has provided would you like to try this week? How will you put it into action?

How can you begin to share with your friends about Jesus? What might be a couple of first steps to take?

Who are people you know or have heard about whose lives have been changed by their friendship with Jesus? Write down a few of these stories. How could you use these stories to begin to share with others about Jesus?

If you can't think of any stories from your own life or from the lives of others you know, check out these true accounts from the Bible. Maybe you haven't had an experience as dramatic as one of these stories, but God's still just as powerful today and can still change lives!

- Acts 9:26-42
- Philemon
- Acts 16:25-34

DO THIS AT HOME THIS WEEK

When sharing our faith, it's important to think about what we actually believe. It helps to write out thoughts ahead of time to make sure you've thought this through and know what you want to say. Get yourself ready to share your faith by taking some time to write your thoughts about each of these questions. When sharing your faith, it is important that you understand what you truly believe and what you know to be true. Take some time to write down:

What do I believe about God?

What do I know is true about God?

What am I not sure about?

Who can I talk to this week to help me understand the things I don't know?

Take time to read and reflect on "Be Bold!" in the Bonus section of this book.

PRAYER TIME

- Pray that the Lord will deepen your love for Him and for others so that you'll be motivated to share with them.
- Ask God to open up conversations where you'll have the opportunity to tell others about your faith.
- Thank God for sending Jesus and for what He has already done in your life.

MEMORY VERSE

My grace is all you need. My power works best in weakness.
(2 Corinthians 12:9)

God's Story and My Story

>> Instead, you must worship Christ as Lord of your life. And if someone asks about your Christian hope, always be ready to explain it. (1 Peter 3:15)

everyone loves a good story

The Bible is packed with amazing stories. Jesus was a master storyteller. Even today, few people can pass up a movie or book that tells a good story. So it makes sense that using stories can help us share about Jesus. We're going to work through a process that will help you use stories too. Here's a quick overview of what that looks like:

- *God's story and my story*: We share what God has done and is doing in our lives.
- *My story and your story*: As we're authentic with others in sharing our story, we make ourselves available to listen to their stories.
- *Your story and God's story*: As we listen to their stories, we are able to help them discover how God reaches out to them.

The Bible is full of stories. Our Lord was a master storyteller, as the parables show. The word *parable* is the translation of two Greek terms that mean "to throw alongside of." Frank H. Seilhamer says, "What is involved here is a story created to be thrown alongside of a true-life situation to drive home the central point the storyteller is trying to make. As Jesus demonstrated, a good picture is worth a thousand words that slip by."

Do remember that there are no particular "formulas" for telling others about Jesus. There's no perfect way to present the gospel. Your best tools will always be listening, prayer, and love. This method of using stories is simply a helpful tool.

Also remember that the Holy Spirit does not *make* us share our faith; the Holy Spirit *enables* us to share our faith. The Holy Spirit is already working in the hearts of the people we want to share with. God pursues the people we love, and He'll provide opportunities for us to share Christ.

No matter how we try, we can't *make* people follow Jesus. That's not our job. Instead, our role is to help our friends become interested in finding out about Jesus and then share about Him as appropriately and helpfully as we can, letting God change their hearts and minds. You can trust God for this important job.

As you're sharing stories with your friends, never forget your love for them — as we learned in our last session, love should be our motivation. That means pride, judging, or thinking we know better than others will spoil our story.

my story

Your story is what you've experienced in your own life. When you tell others about your experiences, you're sharing a part of your journey. Part of that journey includes how you came to know Christ and how He is changing you even now.

People today want honest relationships. They're not interested in hearing only about our successes, but they also want to hear about our failures, too; not only our gains, but also our losses; not only our pleasures, but also our pains; not only our hopes, but also our disappointments. When we share all sides of our story, we become more real. This means that telling our story isn't about *selling* something — instead it's about *sharing* together.

What do you usually focus on when you're talking to others? Are you open and honest about both the good and the bad? Your ups and your downs?

People are looking for love and acceptance, not just words. Many times what we *do* is much more important than what we *say*.

Do your words and actions work together to tell about the love of Jesus? What are three things you could do to improve in this area?

People are looking to see your faith lived out in front of them. This is taking actions a step further — so it's not just a few random acts of kindness, but your whole life. People are looking for those who live the talk — whose lives reflect what they are saying. They want to see Jesus in us!

How does your whole life reflect the love of Jesus? What are areas of your life that might not be giving people a good picture of Jesus and His love?

God's story in your story

You wouldn't carry on a conversation with a new acquaintance for long without mentioning your best friend. How could you avoid talking about that person, why you like him or her, what you enjoy doing together, and so on? In the same way, you can't tell your story without God's story being included. This, of course, assumes that you have a real and growing relationship with Jesus. If you don't, then it will be difficult to include God in your story.

You'd probably say you're *dedicated* or *devoted* to your best friends. This means you feel strongly about your friendship, that you're committed to those friends, and perhaps you'd even go to great lengths to keep the friendships alive.

Who are people you are dedicated or devoted to?

If God is a key part of your life, you'll demonstrate that same kind of dedication or devotion to Him as well. And this will be reflected in your story. The life of Jesus (His story!) gives us examples of what it means to be dedicated or devoted to God. Let's take a look:

silence and solitude

Jesus demonstrated devotion through His prayer life. He often left the crowds and prayed alone, or He would gather with His close followers to pray.

Read Luke 5:16 for one example of this. Where do you like to go to get away and pray?

scripture and study

Jesus knew God's Word, and was able to use it in His teachings and His discussions with both friends and enemies. Do you think He knew it all by heart because He is God? Or do you think He had to study it as a young man? Either way, He showed his devotion through knowing God's Word.

Read 2 Timothy 3:16-17. What does this passage tell you about the importance of God's Word?

surrender

Jesus demonstrated His devotion by giving His life. He died on the cross so that we could have a relationship with God. He must have really trusted God's plan to be willing to go through that suffering!

Are there things you may have to give up or surrender to God to demonstrate your devotion to Him? What might be gained by your actions?

Remember, nothing can take the place of a close and authentic friendship with Jesus Christ! That's where God's story and your story join together!

DO THIS AT HOME THIS WEEK

- Spend some time in quiet reflection, looking at some of the Bible verses from this session. Write down your thoughts and feelings during these times of reflection.
- Quietly consider your friendship with Jesus. How are you helping that friendship to grow? How are you demonstrating your devotion to that relationship?

- Write down some examples from your life where God's story has overlapped and become a part of your story.
- Read "What it Means to Believe in Jesus" on pages 99-100 of this book. This will help you understand more deeply what it means for someone to accept Jesus as Lord and Savior.

PRAYER TIME

- Ask the Lord to guide you as you honestly think through your story.
- Pray for opportunities to grow in your relationship with God.
- Praise Jesus for what He's done in your life!

MEMORY VERSE

Instead, you must worship Christ as Lord of your life. And if someone asks about your Christian hope, always be ready to explain it. (1 Peter 3:15)

My Story and Your Story

>> So, my dear brothers and sisters, be strong and immovable. Always work enthusiastically for the Lord, for you know that nothing you do for the Lord is ever useless. (1 Corinthians 15:58)

We all have a desire to be heard. Unfortunately, because so much of life is busy and noisy, we often live in a world of isolation and secrets. Most of us want someone to listen to us in a safe, non-judgmental way. Most people are looking for friends who have enough time and patience to hear their story, friends who won't change their mind and abandon a friendship once those stories are shared. During this session we're going to focus on listening to others and learning what their stories are all about.

Before we get started, though, a quick reminder. No one wants to be someone else's "project." Remember back to our first session — our motivation is love. That love moves us to reach out in friendship — not because of our desire to meet an evangelistic goal. Relationships should be built on respect, mutual trust, shared experiences, and equal status.

sharing my story

During our last session you had the opportunity to think about your own story, and how your story and God's story overlap. Now it's time to think about how to share that story with someone else. Here are two important tips:

1. *Be real.* Don't make up or embellish what's happening in your life to sound more spiritual. Just be yourself! Your life is a testimony or example to others who are watching you and getting to know you better. Of course, you want to do your best to be a great example, but you also don't want to come across as a big phony.

Does your life honor God and make others curious about getting to know Him? Read Ephesians 4:1. What encouragement or guidance do you get from this verse?

2. *Depend on Jesus.* God may not want you to tell the whole story at one time. He may want you to share it over a period of days or weeks or even months. This is why a continued relationship is so important. Allow the Holy Spirit to guide you through your conversations.

Read Hebrews 12:1-3 and write your thoughts about what it says here.

discovering their story

While you're sharing your story (remember, this can take weeks to do), you'll also be getting to know the other person—discovering his or her story. This means you're going to need to spend time with that person. Be available to him or her. And, if you haven't been reminded enough, here it is again: Love that person! Your motivation for spending time and discovering that person's story is love.

It seems like common sense, but amazingly many people forget that the best way to learn someone else's story is to listen. It sounds so basic . . . but listening is one of the most important ways you can get to know someone else.

Most of us aren't that great at listening (perhaps we're just too busy talking!). Here are four great skills to help you become a better listener.

1. *"The onion principle."* An onion is peeled one layer at a time. Each layer that comes off takes you closer and closer to the center of the onion. It's the same with people. They need to trust you before they're going to start opening up and letting those layers peel away. Let others know they can trust you through your words and your actions. Don't gossip about what is shared with you or use information in any other inappropriate manner. No one will share their story with you if they feel unsafe around you, and some secrets are too scary to tell right away. With time and trust they'll reveal the layers that lead to their hearts.

When have you tried to rush a friendship? What happened? Think about a friendship that you've had a long time—what did it take to develop trust in that relationship?

2. *Ask questions that don't have question marks.* Instead of grilling someone with a list of questions, make conversation more natural by saying things such as:

- Tell me more about your family.
- I'd like to hear more about that.
- I'd love to know more about your hobbies or things you do in your spare time.
- Tell me how that's working out for you.

This is a more gentle approach to encouraging someone to share with you. Ask tough questions gently.

What are a few other questions without question marks that you could use to get to know someone better? Can you think of three?

3. *Pause.* When someone else is talking, are you already thinking about what you're going to say next instead of listening to them? Do you feel nervous if there's a bit of quiet before someone answers a question? Remember, some people listen only long enough to think of something to say. If you've got two people like this in a conversation, it's really just a competition for airtime — and no one is listening at all! Always give people time to speak and be heard. Pause your own talking long enough for others to have a turn.

Ask someone a question, and then wait until that person has answered completely. No interrupting allowed! Is this hard or easy for you? How can you improve in this skill?

4. *Be a caring listener.* When someone is talking, show you're listening by doing a few of these things:

- Maintain eye contact. If you're looking in the other direction, it's clear that you're distracted.
- Lean toward the person.
- If it's appropriate, touch the other person.
- Respond appropriately. If they're sharing something sad, be empathetic. If they're excited, share that moment of celebration.

What actions make you feel that someone else is listening to you? What makes you feel like others are not listening?

DO THIS AT HOME THIS WEEK

- Choose one of the four listening skills to practice. Choose the one that's hardest and write down a few notes on how you're improving.
- List two people you'd like to get to know better. What's one thing you can do this week to get to know each of these people's stories?
- Write down the important parts of your own story. This isn't just the part where you came to know Jesus. It also includes how God has used hard times to help you grow, how God has given guidance, prayers that have been answered, and so on.
- After you've written down these key parts of your story, reflect on these questions:

1. Could another person get to know the real me from these stories? Are they true and real?

2. Is there a connection between these stories and my relationship with Jesus?

Reaching Out

3. Do the stories show that God is doing something in my life?

PRAYER TIME

- Spend some time thanking the Lord for unexpected opportunities to share about Him with those around you.
- Ask God to help you be a better listener. Take time to listen to God, too!

MEMORY VERSE

So, my dear brothers and sisters, be strong and immovable. Always work enthusiastically for the Lord, for you know that nothing you do for the Lord is ever useless. (1 Corinthians 15:58)

God's Story and Your Story

>> But to all who believed him and accepted him, he gave the right to become children of God. (John 1:12)

This session helps us introduce our friends to the possibility that God is already present and working in their lives. Let's look at four stages in our relationships that may help us as we try to be available to God and His plans.

1. Notice God's footprints in people's stories.
2. Continue going deeper in conversations with others.
3. Discover where you can meet people's practical, everyday needs.
4. Follow Christ and focus on prayer.

These aren't "four easy steps." Instead, these are four stages that can help introduce a human friend to our heavenly friend. Sometimes the stages may occur simultaneously or out of sequence. At other times the process might occur in the order shown here. Sometimes it happens in one conversation; sometimes it takes years. The point is that there's no fool-proof formula.

1. *Notice God's footprints in people's stories.* God is already working in the life of your friend—but it's very likely your friend has not noticed this or has attributed the work of God to something else, such as being a good person,

luck, or another religious philosophy. As you spend time with your friend, look for God's "footprints" in that person's life — evidence that God is already at work. You might notice:

- A spiritual sensitivity in the person
- A desire to experience spirituality or your friend exploring spiritual topics
- A longing to be different or for change in his or her life
- After making a mistake, your friend wants to start over again

As you notice these things and draw attention to them in your friend's life, remember to be gentle and respectful, just as Peter expresses in 1 Peter 3:15-16.

2. *Continue going deeper in conversations with others.* As you listen to your friend's story and get to know him or her better, think about parallels you see in your friend's life that relate to Jesus' story. Keep in mind:

- You don't have to do it all in one conversation. In fact, it's likely to take many conversations and many shared experiences.
- You don't have to do it the same way every time. Remember, people in the Bible shared about Jesus in a lot of different ways, depending on the people they were talking to and the circumstances.
- You don't have to have all the answers. How *could* you have all the answers? Just share from your heart and be willing to say, "I don't know, but I'll find out." And then be sure you talk to someone who can help you find out.

You might also find it helpful to think of real-life situations that can illustrate a Bible concept. These might help your friend understand a concept related to having a friendship with Jesus in terms that are easier to understand. For example:

- We often read in the news about hostage situations where someone is held for ransom. Jesus paid the ransom for us so we are not held hostage to sin. Jesus "redeemed" us.
- Many of us have occasion to go to court, or we watch courtroom movies and television shows. By His death and resurrection, Jesus

- made us not guilty. He pardoned us. This is called "justification."
- Families or couples who are torn apart often try to work things out. We have been torn apart from God by sin. Jesus made things right and brought God and us together. This is called "reconciliation."
- Accounts of someone giving a kidney or other body part amaze us because of the donor's sacrifice. We even read of people who jump in front of a bullet or a moving car, sacrificing their own lives so someone else can live. Jesus sacrificed or gave Himself for us, and this is called "propitiation."

What are other examples from real life that you might use to help someone else understand what Jesus has done?

There are many natural occurrences in life that can also be used in conversations as you or your friend move through them. Think of a time you or your friend experienced one or more of these situations, and write a way your conversation about that situation might lead to a discussion of Jesus.

Your favorite team winning

The birth of a child

A wedding

Getting to meet someone you look up to (government official, athlete/sports figure, actor, celebrity, etc.)

Going on a journey or road trip

Reaching a milestone, such as graduation or a promotion at work

3. *Discover where you can meet people's practical, everyday needs.* One of the most basic truths about Jesus is that He walked among people with compassion, healing them and meeting their physical needs.

Jesus met real needs of real people. In the same way, if we are not caring for people in need, we're not representing Jesus well. This is a big challenge for many Christians. We can talk about Jesus, but our actions may not support our words very well. With repeated acts of compassion born from a deep love and appreciation of God's world and His people, we can bring light into seemingly hopeless and dark situations.

What are three things you could do this week that would meet a real and practical need of a friend? This might be giving a ride to someone, babysitting for free, secretly leaving groceries on a doorstep, or any of hundreds of other ideas. What will you choose to do?

4. *Follow Christ and focus on prayer.* As we've noted before, we can't force anyone to follow Jesus — others are responsible for their own actions. We can follow Christ and pray. Ask God to give you wisdom about what to do, what to say, and when to say it. Ask God to renew your excitement about your friendship with Him.

Often simply being grateful and thankful helps us be an inspiring example for others.

DO THIS AT HOME THIS WEEK

- Take time to read and reflect on "Evangelism Is Important" on pages 101-102 of this book.
- What are two stories from your life that can relate to what Jesus has done by His death and resurrection? How can you share these with a friend who is going through a similar situation in his or her own life?
- Remember the three things you wrote that you could do to meet the needs of someone? Do them!

Reaching Out

PRAYER TIME

Ask the Lord to direct you to people you can serve and share Jesus with. Ask Him to give them open hearts to His love and to your words and actions.

MEMORY VERSE

> But to all who believed him and accepted him, he gave the right to become children of God. (John 1:12)

Friendship Evangelism

> > For I am not ashamed of this Good News about Christ.
> It is the power of God at work, saving everyone who
> believes—the Jew first and also the Gentile. (Romans 1:16)

Friendship evangelism means making real and deep friendships with people while living in a way that honors God and lets His love show through you. Through our friendships we model the life of a Jesus-follower with the hope that our friends will want to get to know Jesus and serve Him as we do.

Evangelism doesn't just happen. It is a process that takes time and effort on our part. Relationships are not always easy, and we must be prepared to give our time and commitment to those God has put into our lives. In Ephesians 5.16-17 Paul says, "Make the most of every opportunity in these evil days. Don't act thoughtlessly, but understand what the Lord wants you to do." God wants to use us in every stage of our deepening friendships. Evangelism largely depends on the depth of our relationship with each friend and with Jesus.

The stages of growing friendships are:

- Meeting and getting to know others. This goes beyond just being introduced, shaking hands, and sharing a bit of small talk. This is

Reaching Out

when you meet someone and connect. You want to be friends. This means you want to hear the other person, get to know him or her, and begin to trust each other. This takes time.
- Showing the real me. If you only let friends see the "perfect" version of you, they'll never know the real you. Letting our friends see Christ living in us, along with our mistakes and failures, is a part of that. Showing and sharing what makes our lives different is important too.
- Being there for them. Helping a friend respond to his or her life issues with God's perspective is important. The Bible tells us in Ephesians 5:2 that we should "Live a life filled with love, following the example of Christ. He loved us and offered himself as a sacrifice for us." There is often sacrifice in helping out a friend in need.

the example of Jesus

Let's look at an account from the life of Jesus that can help us see what friendship evangelism might look like for us. Read John 4:1-43 and then reflect on these questions:

By being a Samaritan, this woman was despised by Jews (which Jesus and His disciples were). Because of her many partners, she was the subject of gossip in her town. She was a complete outcast. From this story and others you know from the Bible, how did Jesus act around people whom others had cast aside?

Jesus moved from talking about a physical need (water) to a spiritual need (living water). How can we use a similar comparison from our own lives to open doors of conversation?

What could you learn from this account that might help you in sharing your faith with a friend? List three things.

practical ideas

If you struggle with thinking of ways to show you care, here are ideas you can use. Let these spark new ideas for you. Be creative!

Do something kind without expecting anything in return:

- Help with a chore your friend hates to do.
- Share food with a hungry friend.
- Invite your friend over to hang out.
- Visit your friend when he or she is sick or needs encouragement.

Who can I be kind to this week? What will I do?

Say something encouraging:

- Compliment your friend—and mean it!
- If you feel funny saying something nice out loud, write a note and say it there.

Reaching Out

- Defend your friend when others are being unfair or unkind.
- Help your friend to think positively when a situation is discouraging.

Who can I encourage with words this week? What will I say?

Listen:

- Help your friend feel that what he or she has to say is important.
- Focus on your friend's needs rather than on your needs.

Who needs me to listen especially well this week?

Find out what's important to your friend:

- What questions does your friend have about God? The future? Right and wrong?
- What painful experiences has your friend gone through? A broken home? Painful relationships? Disappointment?
- What fears does your friend have? A problem without a solution? A health issue they or a loved one may have? Financial troubles?
- What's going well in your friend's life? A recent accomplishment? A meaningful relationship?

Who is a friend I don't know much about? How can I learn more about this friend in a gentle, non-threatening way? What questions should I ask?

DO THIS AT HOME THIS WEEK

Take a friendship to the next level. This week, think of two people you've met but don't know very well. Write their names below.

Your assignment this week is to:

1. Find out what these two people care about.
2. Do something to show each of them that you care about them.
3. Think about those same two friends. Where would you say you are in the stages of friendship discussed earlier in this session? How could you take these relationships to the next stage?
4. Read the poem, "What a Friend" below, and then write your own poem that reflects your friendship with Jesus.

What a Friend

It was one gloomy morning
The fishermen sat idly on their boats
A dreary day, nothing to celebrate
Right there on the lake of Gennesaret.

And broken and tired they were
Then they saw the crowd, milling around him
A friend of the broken hearted
As by the shore, He shared the message of hope.

Hope! Any hope for us?
After a whole night of unfruitful toil?
He speaks hope, can't he see?
Maybe it's time to down tools and quit.

The teacher spoke; such love, such warmth
Gentle, sure, firmer than the mountains
He spoke, words of power
Was it a joke, commanding such impossibility?

Reaching Out

"Put out into the deep water, let down the nets for a catch."
The big fisherman obeyed, doubting all the while
Then all went wrong. All right?
What's happening, the nets were breaking!

Too good to be true; is this for real?
The fish, for volume, tilted the boat
Fear and awe gripped the hearts of the fishermen
"Don't be afraid," he said.
"From now on, you'll catch men."

What power! They packed up,
Abandoned their nets and followed him . . .

—Ken Aringo

PRAYER TIME

- Thank God for each of your friends.
- Pray for wisdom as God leads you to share about Him with your friends.

MEMORY VERSE

For I am not ashamed of this Good News about Christ. It is the power of God at work, saving everyone who believes—the Jew first and also the Gentile. (Romans 1:16)

Prayer Evangelism

> > Jesus traveled through all the towns and villages of that area, teaching in the synagogues and announcing the Good News about the Kingdom. And he healed every kind of disease and illness. When he saw the crowds, he had compassion on them because they were confused and helpless, like sheep without a shepherd. He said to his disciples, "The harvest is great, but the workers are few. So pray to the Lord who is in charge of the harvest; ask him to send more workers into his fields." (Matthew 9:35-38)

As a farmer understands, the most important time to have plenty of workers is when the crops are ready for harvest. If there are not enough workers, then the harvesting season will pass and the crop will be lost. Jesus uses this analogy of the harvest to help us understand that there are many people in need of Jesus, but not enough "workers" to tell them of Jesus.

What do we do? Jesus tells us to pray.

Jesus wants us to share His message with our friends. Praying for them is the best place to begin. Intercession—praying to God on behalf of another person—is a way to reach others. Jesus said in John 6:63, "The Spirit alone gives eternal life. Human effort accomplishes nothing." And in verse 44, he says, "For no one can come to me unless the Father who sent me draws them to me."

Prayer, therefore, is critical. Let's explore how we can pray effectively for our friends to come to know Jesus.

Pray faithfully. God could use any means to convince people to believe in Him if He wanted. Instead, He's chosen *us* to reach out to His people. Don't become discouraged and stop praying—pray regularly for those who don't know Jesus.

Rely on God's power. The Bible indicates that we're in a spiritual battle with the powers of darkness. Satan wants us to fail. First Peter 5:8 and Ephesians 5:10-20 let us know we're involved in spiritual warfare. Prayer is our weapon, and God has the power to win this battle.

Invest time in others. Show that you take your friendships with others seriously by spending time in prayer for them. Set aside time each day to pray for your friends.

Encourage others to pray. Meet with friends and pray for those you know who aren't followers of Jesus. Matthew 18:19-20 tells us there is power in group prayer. (We'll follow up on this more deeply in our next session.)

Never give up! Our job is to pray. God is in control of all the results. We can be encouraged and thankful for whatever He brings us. Patience and faithfulness are fruit of the Spirit (see Galatians 5:22-23).

Look for opportunities. As you pray, be ready for and available to God's leading. At the appropriate time, God will offer opportunities. Watch for them. Colossians 4:5-6 tells us to "Live wisely among those who are not believers, and make the most of every opportunity. Let your conversation be gracious and attractive so that you will have the right response for everyone."

what the bible says about praying for others

Read Colossians 1:9-14. List as many things as you see in these verses that we should be praying for.

Read Ephesians 6:18. What does this passage help you understand about the importance of prayer?

Read John 17, where Jesus prays for His followers. What does Jesus specifically ask for us?

Read 1 Timothy 2:1-8. What new insights on prayer can you gain from these verses?

From what the Bible says about prayer, what role does prayer play in evangelism?

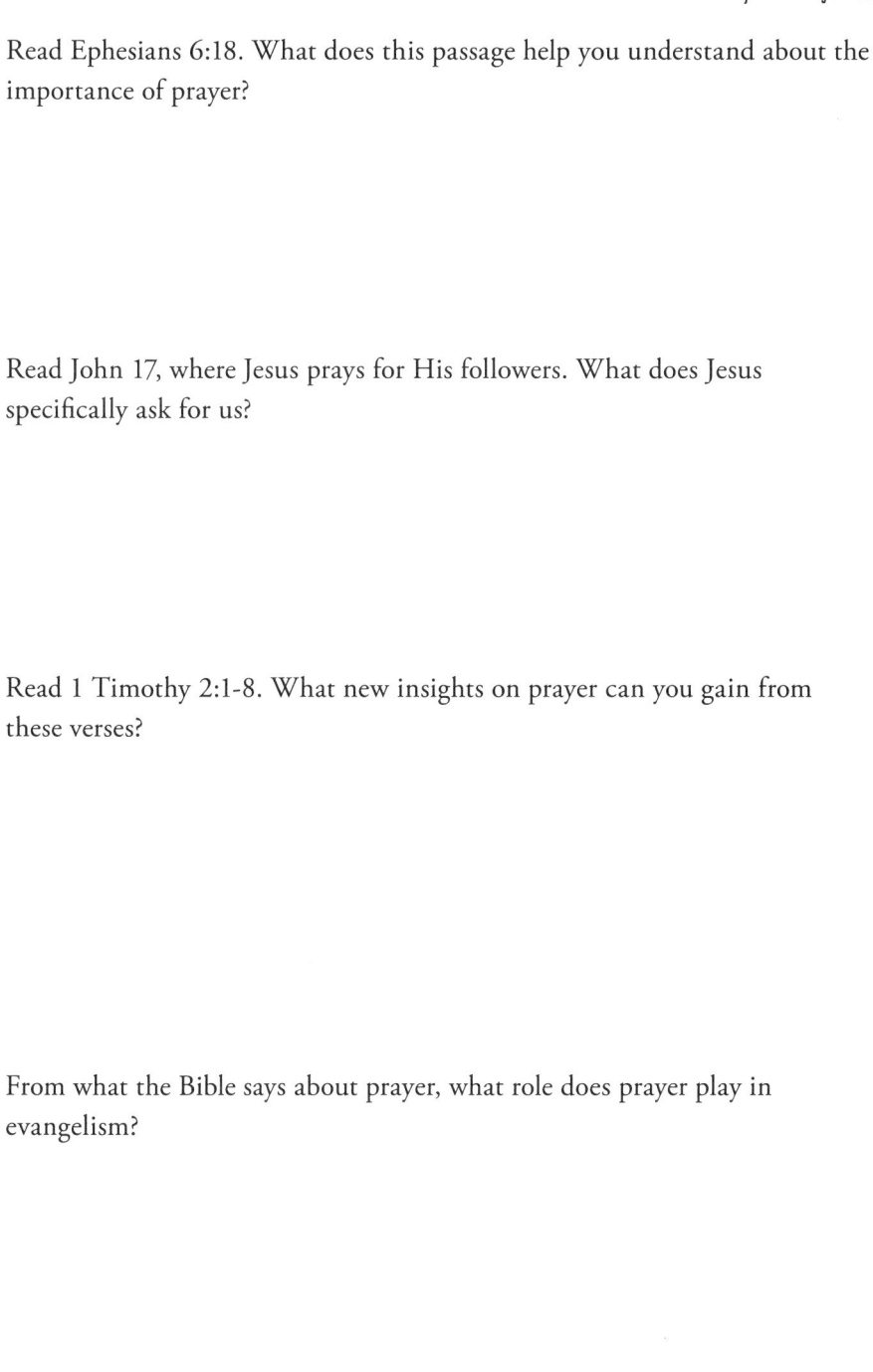

practical prayer ideas

Here are a few ideas of how to begin:

- Write the names of a few friends on an index card. Keep it in your pocket or notebook to remind you to pray for them.
- Pray through the alphabet. Start praying for specific friends whose names begin with that letter of the alphabet. Skip a letter if no one comes to mind.
- Pray with other Christians. Gather a few friends who follow Jesus and pray for those you want to share Jesus with. Meet at break time or after school.
- Keep a journal. God answers prayers. Keep a record of your prayers and God's answers in your journal.
- Take a prayer walk in your area. Pray for your friends as you walk by where they live, work, or go to school.
- Pray when you see your friends. As you see people, silently take a moment to pray to God for them.

DO THIS AT HOME THIS WEEK

- Choose two of the ideas above that you'll do this week. Get started now!

PRAYER TIME

- Thank the Lord for the friends He's given you and the privilege you have to pray for friends who don't follow Jesus.
- Pray that the Holy Spirit will bring to your mind others to pray for.

MEMORY VERSE

Devote yourselves to prayer with an alert mind and a thankful heart. Pray for us, too, that God will give us many opportunities to speak about his mysterious plan concerning Christ. That is why I am here in chains. (Colossians 4:2-3)

Prayer Groups

>> I also tell you this: If two of you agree here on earth concerning anything you ask, my Father in heaven will do it for you. For where two or three gather together as my followers, I am there among them. (Matthew 18:19-20)

In our previous session we discussed the importance of prayer in sharing the love and message of Jesus with others. This session will take that idea much deeper by giving you guidance on starting a prayer group. We're going to have a little fun with this and make everything use the number three. You might want to name your prayer group triplets, trios, triangles, troikas, or another word that relates to the number three.

what's a prayer group?

A prayer group involves a team of three Jesus-followers committed to praying together regularly for friends who don't yet follow Jesus and for the spiritual needs of other countries. Three friends agree to meet for thirty minutes on a weekly basis to pray for three friends each (nine friends total) who don't follow Jesus, plus one country of their choice (a total of three). Begin with a three-month commitment to pray together and, after that, renew the commitment.

Reaching Out

How to Start a Prayer Group

Step 1. Find two friends who will commit to join with you to pray for friends who need Jesus and for the spiritual needs of other nations. Why are we suggesting you find two friends so you'll have three in your group? Jesus made some specific promises to pairs and trios who pray. Check out Matthew 18:19-20 and Ecclesiastes 4:12.

Write the names of your prayer group members here.

Step 2. Each group member should write down the names of three friends who don't follow Jesus.

Step 3. Decide on a day, time (set aside thirty minutes), and place to meet.

Write that down here. Also write down contact info for those in your group in case you need to reschedule.

Step 4. Use the following guide to assist you during your time of prayer. This is only a suggestion for how to pray. God may lead you to pray differently. Always follow His leading!

Prayer Group Guide

1. *Pray for spiritual renewal for yourselves and for your churches.* The goal is to pray that each person in your group will get to know Jesus better and become more like Him. After this your focus can switch to the renewal of the body of Christ in your city and country.

Worship:

- Praise God for His greatness!
- Read a psalm that tells of God's character, or sing a praise song.
- Thank God for what He means to you and what He has done for you.
- Thank God for the great privilege of praying.

Prayer for one another:

- Pray that each of you will become more like Jesus.
- Pray that each of you will have personal and family needs met.
- Pray that your churches will be healthy places where people meet Jesus and grow in relationship with Him.
- Ask God to empower you and your friends to share His love wherever He has put you.
- Ask God to use each of you to share with your three friends.

2. *Pray for the salvation of your friends.* Each member should pray for three friends who don't follow Jesus. This means that the team will be praying, by name, for nine people. Remember what we've learned about praying for people who don't know Jesus. Begin by asking God to intervene in the lives of your friends, drawing them to Jesus. Then boldly declare that no weapon of Satan will prosper. Pray against Satan's plans in the name of Jesus. Also pray that your friends will be shielded from Satan's lies and temptations.

Pray that your nine friends . . .

- will come to a personal relationship with Jesus and be saved from the punishment of sin (Romans 10:1).
- will be drawn to Jesus (John 6:44).
- will not be blinded from the truth by Satan or the world (2 Corinthians 4:4).
- will seek to know God (Acts 17:27).
- will be convicted of their wrong deeds and guided in all truth by the Holy Spirit (John 16:8,13).
- will repent of their disobedience and turn to God (Acts 3:19).
- will long for a relationship with Christ (John 7:37-38).

Reaching Out

3. *Pray for the world.* The group should pray for the worldwide work of God. The team should choose three countries toward which to focus their prayers. The more you know about these countries, the more clearly you can pray.

- Pray for those who have not yet heard of Jesus and His death and resurrection, that God would draw them to His Son (John 6:44).
- Ask for God's blessing, peace, protection, encouragement, and growth in the lives of Christians within the three countries you've chosen (especially if these are countries where Christians are persecuted), and that the Holy Spirit will enable them to fulfill their purpose in Jesus (Colossians 1:9-14; Psalm 5:11; Psalm 10:17; Philippians 2:13; Philippians 4:6-7; Titus 2:11-14).
- Pray for those in leadership of these countries. Pray that they would . . .
  - glorify God (Psalm 138:4-5).
  - act with God's wisdom (Daniel 2:20).
  - follow Jesus (Mark 2:14).
  - uphold righteousness (Isaiah 11:2-4).
  - hear God's Word (Acts 13:7).
  - walk in integrity (Proverbs 20:28).
  - love their families (Psalm 115:14).

DO THIS AT HOME THIS WEEK

Establish a prayer group and report the names of those in your group to your leader. Share when you're meeting and where so you can be held accountable.

PRAYER TIME

- Pray that the Lord will help your prayer life to grow into a powerful ministry.
- Ask the Lord to guide you as you seek to intercede for others.
- Praise the Lord that you can come to Him in prayer and that He always hears you.

MEMORY VERSE

I also tell you this: If two of you agree here on earth concerning anything you ask, my Father in heaven will do it for you. For where two or three gather together as my followers, I am there among them. (Matthew 18:19-20)

Power Evangelism

>> But you will receive power when the Holy Spirit comes upon you. And you will be my witnesses, telling people about me everywhere—in Jerusalem, throughout Judea, in Samaria, and to the ends of the earth. (Acts 1:8)

"Power evangelism" refers to sharing the message of God's love by the power and might of God's Holy Spirit. In this way, the Holy Spirit moves in sovereign, supernatural abilities, sometimes with amazing results. These often lead people to accept the gift of salvation and give their lives to Jesus. In fact, 1 Corinthians 4:20 says, "For the Kingdom of God is not just a lot of talk; it is living by God's power."

the power of Jesus' ministry

In the New Testament, *power* means authority. Jesus had all authority given to Him by His Father (Matthew 28:18). He gave authority to His followers (that's us!) to become children of God (John 1:12) and to share in His work (Mark 3:15). Let's look at examples of power as shown by Jesus' ministry.

- Jesus began His ministry in Galilee in the power of the Spirit (Luke 4:14).

Reaching Out

- Jesus did miracles of healing in the power of the Spirit (Luke 5:17).
- Jesus did mighty works in the power of the Spirit (Matthew 11:20).

List some things that Jesus did in His three years of ministry in the power of the Spirit. If you need help, look in Matthew, Mark, Luke, and John (the Gospels).

Read John 14:12. What does this mean to you?

The word that comes to mind after reading John 14:12 is *unbelievable*. Jesus said we would be doing greater works than Him, but not until after He left to be with the Father. Then He would send the Spirit.

In other words, Jesus' ascension into heaven enabled the present ministry of the Holy Spirit in the world (the conviction of sin, repentance, and righteousness), so that salvation in Jesus Christ might be made known everywhere on earth.

Take a look at Jesus' last words in Mark 16:15 and Acts 1:8. What does Jesus want of us?

Would you agree that the very last words spoken from a person who is leaving this life would be very important words to remember? Why or why not? What does this mean when you consider the last words of Jesus here on earth?

the power of God shown through Jesus' followers

Remember, Jesus didn't leave us to do His work without help. He also didn't leave us powerless. Jesus sent the Holy Spirit to live inside us all so that He could continue His work through us. To better understand the power of the Holy Spirit, we can look in the book of Acts. The dominating theme of Acts is the activity of the Holy Spirit. The detailed progress of the spread of the gospel from Jerusalem to Rome can be an encouragement to us as we see our inadequacy in spreading the gospel to all the earth, and yet, see the awesome power of God to do just that.

Read Acts 1 and 2. List three examples from these chapters that show the Holy Spirit works in powerful ways through Christians to reach others for Christ.

WARNING! WARNING! Unfortunately, some of us might seek power for the wrong reasons. This could be destructive to our faith and relationship with Jesus. A man named Simon did this in the Bible. Read his story in Acts 8:18-24. Think about Matthew 16:26 and how it relates to Simon's story.

The book of Acts shows the followers of Jesus spreading His message through both words and actions. They were preaching and teaching the truth, they were demonstrating power that was given to them by the Holy Spirit, and they had bold assurance as they acted with deep conviction.

DO THIS AT HOME THIS WEEK

Spend time writing about ways you've seen God's Spirit working in power to reach people . . .

- Through your life.
- Through your church.
- Through the Spirit working in the lives of others you know.

PRAYER TIME

- Pray that the Lord will empower you with His Spirit to share the love of Jesus in power, boldness, and action.
- Praise the Lord for helping you understand the need for the Holy Spirit's power.
- Ask the Holy Spirit to empower and teach you to be Christ's ambassador to the world, beginning where you live.

MEMORY VERSE

We know, dear brothers and sisters, that God loves you and has chosen you to be his own people. For when we brought you the Good News, it was not only with words but also with power, for the Holy Spirit gave you full assurance that what we said was true. And you know of our concern for you from the way we lived when we were with you. (1 Thessalonians 1:4-5)

Who We Are in God's Eyes

>> Jesus replied, "You must love the Lord your God with all your heart, all your soul, and all your mind." This is the first and greatest commandment. A second is equally important: "Love your neighbor as yourself." (Matthew 22:37-39)

God sees each of us as incredibly valuable. As followers of Jesus, we need to see others like He does. No matter what color of skin, what gender, what religion, what nationality, or what social status, God sees us all the same—through eyes of love. The Bible says in Romans 2:11, "For God does not show favoritism." Therefore, what God sees in each of us is a person created in His image.

We can grow to see people as God sees them and love them as He does. As we learn to see people from God's point of view, we can learn how the Lord would have us involved in others' lives.

Reaching Out

a look at what the bible says

Look at what Scripture shows us about how God sees others and us.

Read Genesis 1:26-27. What was God's intention in creating people?

Read Genesis 9:6. Why does God say you should value human life?

Read Psalm 139:13-16. What are some of the statements that show how valuable people are to God?

Read Romans 3:23 and 6:23. What does God say is true for all of us? As you read these verses together, what is clearly true for all of us? What is the way to avoid the penalty of being eternally separated from God?

Read Genesis 3:1-19. This tells of when people first rebelled. How did this rebellion affect Adam, Eve, and the world they lived in? Find specific examples from this section of Genesis.

Many of our difficulties today are a result of Adam and Eve's choice to disobey God. As a follower of Jesus, you have a responsibility to serve others by helping them face difficulties and, ultimately, help them to know Christ and be forgiven for disobedience and rebellion.

an illustration of our value

There's a story of a speaker who started off his seminar by holding up a $20 bill in a room filled with people. He asked, "Who would like this $20 bill?" Hands started going up.

He said, "I am going to give this to one of you, but first let me do this." He proceeded to crumple the bill up. He then asked, "Who still wants it?" Still, the hands were up in the air.

"Well," he replied, "what if I do this?" He dropped it on the ground and started to grind it into the floor with his shoe. He picked up the bill, now crumpled and dirty. "Now, who still wants it?" Still hands went in the air.

"My friends, you all have learned a very valuable lesson. No matter what I did to the money, you still wanted it because it did not decrease in value. It was still worth $20. Many times in our lives we are dropped, crumpled, and ground into the dirt by the decisions we make and the circumstances that come our way. We feel that we're worthless, but no matter what has happened or what will happen, we will never lose our value—whether we're dirty or clean, crumpled or finely creased. We are still priceless to those who love us, and especially to God! The worth of our lives comes not in what we do or who we know, but by who we are. We are special; let's never forget it!"

(Author Unknown)

Reaching Out

DO THIS AT HOME THIS WEEK

People are made of body, mind, soul, and spirit. Use a dictionary to help write a definition of each of these words.

Body

Mind

Soul

Spirit

Why do you think God made us so complex? What can you learn about how much God values you by the complexity of your being?

Look in the mirror. While you're staring at yourself, thank God for specific things about yourself. He made you and loves you! Thank Him for what you see, for the qualities you don't see, and for the person He's created you to be.

How does knowing how valuable each of us is to God encourage you to share the message of His love with others?

PRAYER TIME

- Praise the Lord for creating you and loving you with a perfect love.
- Ask the Lord to help you truly understand what it means to love your neighbor as yourself.
- Ask God to help you be gracious to others, just as He has been gracious to you.

MEMORY VERSE

Jesus replied, "'You must love the LORD your God with all your heart, all your soul, and all your mind.' This is the first and greatest commandment. A second is equally important: 'Love your neighbor as yourself.'" (Matthew 22:37-39)

Meeting the Needs of Others

>> He ensures that orphans and widows receive justice. He shows love to the foreigners living among you and gives them food and clothing. So you, too, must show love to foreigners, for you yourselves were once foreigners in the land of Egypt. (Deuteronomy 10:18-19)

Our Father is concerned about all aspects of a person. He is not only concerned about our spiritual welfare, but also about our mind, soul, and body — our whole being. Just as God is concerned about us, He wants to use us to care for others and meet their needs. Social involvement, or meeting the needs of others, honors the Lord and brings blessing to the one who serves. Our social action has the following impact:

- The love of Jesus Christ is shown through our actions.
- The character of Jesus is demonstrated in practical ways to people who do not know Him.
- When we build relationships with others we create opportunities for them to see the Spirit at work and be led to Christ.

God caring for the needs of people

From the very beginning of the world, God has demonstrated concern for the whole person and the needs of people. Look at these verses in Genesis, and see what God created, along with what need that met.

	WHAT DID GOD CREATE OR SAY?	WHAT NEED DID THIS MEET?
Genesis 2:8		
Genesis 2:9		
Genesis 2:10		
Genesis 2:19-20		
Genesis 2:18,21-22		
Genesis 3:21		

Is there any human need that you think God overlooked? If so, what is it?

Jesus as a person

Luke 2:52 tells about the process of Jesus growing up, and says that Jesus grew in wisdom (He grew mentally), stature (He grew physically), favor with God (He grew spiritually), and favor with people (He grew socially). When Jesus grew, all aspects of His being or character had to grow. Since this is true of Jesus, we can be sure that it is true of us as well. We need to grow physically, mentally, socially, and spiritually — and so do those whom God puts in our lives.

If we are helping another person, what are some ways we might be able to help that person . . .

. . . grow mentally?

. . . grow physically?

. . . grow socially?

. . . grow spiritually?

Reaching Out

Jesus caring for the needs of people

Read these passages. What specifically did Jesus do to meet needs in each account? What do these verses show about His concern for all people? What do they show you about Jesus' character?

John 2:1-10

John 6:1-14

John 9:1-41

John 11:1-46

Mark 2:1-12

Read these passages. How do these instruct us to live?

Romans 12:6-11

Galatians 6:9-10

Ephesians 5:1-2

Philippians 2:3-5

Colossians 3:12-15

Which of these passages above presents the biggest challenge to your own life? How can you begin to put these concepts into action?

Reaching Out

why is caring for others so important?

You might be thinking that caring for others is a good idea, but maybe it's something you're just not comfortable with. The Bible makes it clear that caring for others isn't to be a low priority.

Read Matthew 25:34-40 and James 1:27, then answer the questions below.

What areas of involvement are identified in these passages?

What does the Bible say will happen if we do not respond to the needs of others?

What does the Bible say will happen if we do respond to the needs of others?

How do these passages motivate you to do what you can to meet the needs of someone you know — or don't know?

what can i do?

There are many ways that we can be socially involved. Read through these options and ask the Lord how He would have you serve others. If the Lord is leading you to get involved, do it!

Friends. Have you heard someone you know mention a need? Or have you actively been keeping your eyes open, looking out for the needs of those in your school, workplace, or neighborhood? There are certainly people with needs! Perhaps someone is going through difficult times or is lacking food, clothing, or employment. Look for a specific action you can take, and follow through with it.

Community service. It's likely there are countless ways you can get involved by volunteering in your community. You can sort food or clothing at a service agency, read to children, deliver meals to the elderly, visit people in the hospital, and so on. Perhaps your church or another organization in your community is already addressing social concerns and you can easily join in. Your efforts will honor the Lord.

Mission trips. Youth for Christ organizes teams of young people to be involved in social concerns in the local community, throughout the country, and in other countries as well. These teams are called Project Serve teams. Contact your local Youth for Christ representative to see how you can get involved. If Youth for Christ is not nearby, there are many churches and other organizations that plan mission trips. Ask around—you'll certainly find a group that would welcome you.

Emergency relief. Sadly, there is no lack of natural disasters such as earthquakes, hurricanes, fires, and so on. Plus there are countless disasters caused by people, such as mass killings, wars, riots, and more. Regardless of how they occur or when they occur, there is great need. Being a socially involved follower of Jesus means being ready to do your part to respond to those needs. Agencies already exist that respond to these emergencies. Maybe the Lord would lead you to join one of these agencies.

DO THIS AT HOME THIS WEEK

- Take time to read "Go and Do the Same" found on pages 103-104 of this book. Consider what this means to you as you move ahead in serving others.

- Consider what one person, namely you, can do. What needs do you see that you could help meet? How will you take action?
- Re-read the verses from this session and your notes about them. Take time to reflect on how God is leading you to serve Him by serving others. As we've said many times, your motivation should be love. How is God drawing you to show love to others?

PRAYER TIME

- Pray that the Lord will direct you to someone who needs to see God's love made real through you.
- Pray that the Lord will help you not to be self-centered, but that you will be involved in the lives of others.
- Praise the Lord that you have the opportunity to make a difference!

MEMORY VERSE

Work willingly at whatever you do, as though you were working for the Lord rather than for people. Remember that the Lord will give you an inheritance as your reward, and that the Master you are serving is Christ. (Colossians 3:23-24)

Being a Servant Leader (Part 1)

>> Since God chose you to be the holy people he loves, you must clothe yourselves with tenderhearted mercy, kindness, humility, gentleness, and patience. (Colossians 3:12)

Some leaders we see in the world today set themselves apart from the people they lead. Many leaders feel they should have special privileges and live above the people they lead—not having to care about the real needs of the people.

Two disciples of Jesus wanted to be leaders and sit on either side of Jesus in heaven. James and John had their mother pull Jesus aside to ask for this special favor. To answer, Jesus called all the disciples over for a vital lesson in leadership. Here's what He said:

> You know that the rulers in this world lord it over their people, and officials flaunt their authority over those under them. But among you it will be different. Whoever wants to be a leader among you must be your servant, and whoever wants to be first among you must become your slave. For even the Son of Man came not to be served but to serve others and to give his life as a ransom for many. (Matthew 20:25-28)

The kind of leader Jesus wants is a *servant* leader. Servant leaders lead by example and care deeply about the needs of people they lead. They also care deeply for the needs of everyone around them.

During this session and the one that follows, we'll look more closely at what it means to be a servant leader and the characteristics of such a leader.

characteristic 1: servanthood

It may seem obvious that a person who is a servant leader would have a heart of service. Servanthood is serving others sacrificially with God's love. It means putting aside ourselves and being humble enough to go where others aren't willing to go, and do tasks others aren't willing to do. The actions of a servant are motivated by love.

Jesus' example. Jesus gave us a wonderful example of servanthood through His actions in John 13:1-5,12-17. Read this passage and answer the following questions:

How do you think Jesus felt as He was washing His disciples' feet?

Why was Jesus the last person who should have washed those dirty feet?

What are the implications for us based on Jesus' actions and words?

Read these additional verses on servanthood. How are you challenged by these words?

Galatians 5:13

Mark 10:42-45

characteristic 2: willingness to get involved

Jesus isn't looking for people who will sit on the sidelines doing nothing. He wants us to get involved! Read the following passages and note how each of these people rolled up their sleeves and got into the action.

(Note, in each of these accounts there is a much longer and very amazing story. Here we've just provided a nugget. When you have time, read the whole story of each of these people in the Bible and see how God really got involved in their lives.)

Joseph. Read the problem Joseph faced in Genesis 41:54-55. Discover the solution in Genesis 41:47-49,56-57.

What would have happened if Joseph had not gotten involved? What kinds of needs were met through his actions?

Reaching Out

Are you aware of any similar situation going on in the world right now? How is it like or different from this situation and solution?

Nehemiah. Read the problem Nehemiah faced in Nehemiah 2:17. Discover the solution in Nehemiah 2:20, 4:6, and 6:15-16.

What would have happened if Nehemiah had not gotten involved? What kinds of needs were met through his actions?

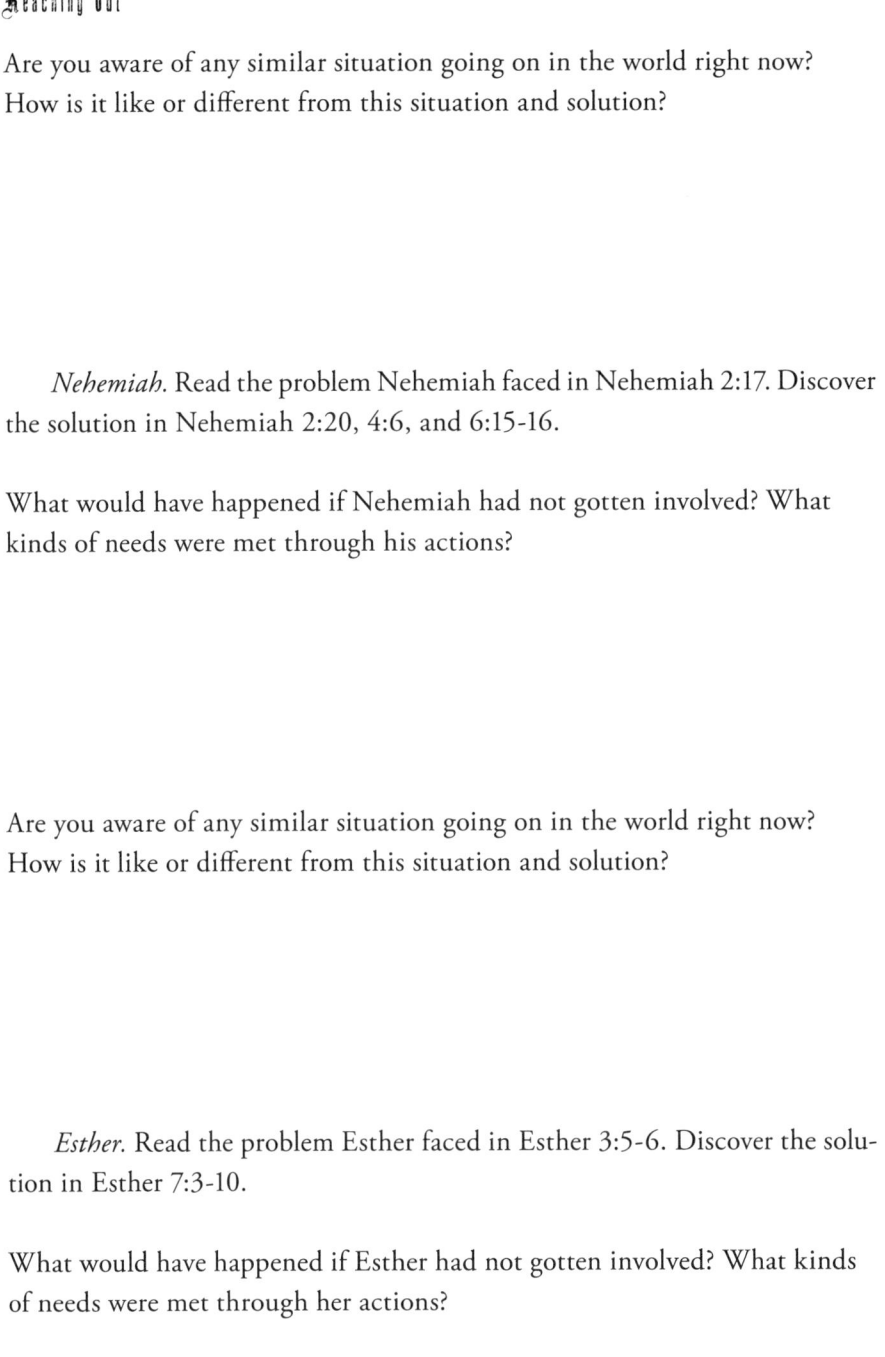

Are you aware of any similar situation going on in the world right now? How is it like or different from this situation and solution?

Esther. Read the problem Esther faced in Esther 3:5-6. Discover the solution in Esther 7:3-10.

What would have happened if Esther had not gotten involved? What kinds of needs were met through her actions?

Are you aware of any similar situation going on in the world right now? How is it like or different from this situation and solution?

characteristic 3: compassion or mercy

A servant leader will have a heart of compassion and mercy. Note that these words are often used interchangeably in the Bible, and have very similar meanings.

How would you define compassion and mercy? Is there a difference between the two? If so, what is it?

God's compassion and mercy. The Bible gives us many examples of God's compassion and mercy.
Read these verses and reflect on them. Write down your insights about God and His compassion and mercy.

Psalm 103:4

Lamentations 3:22-23

Reaching Out

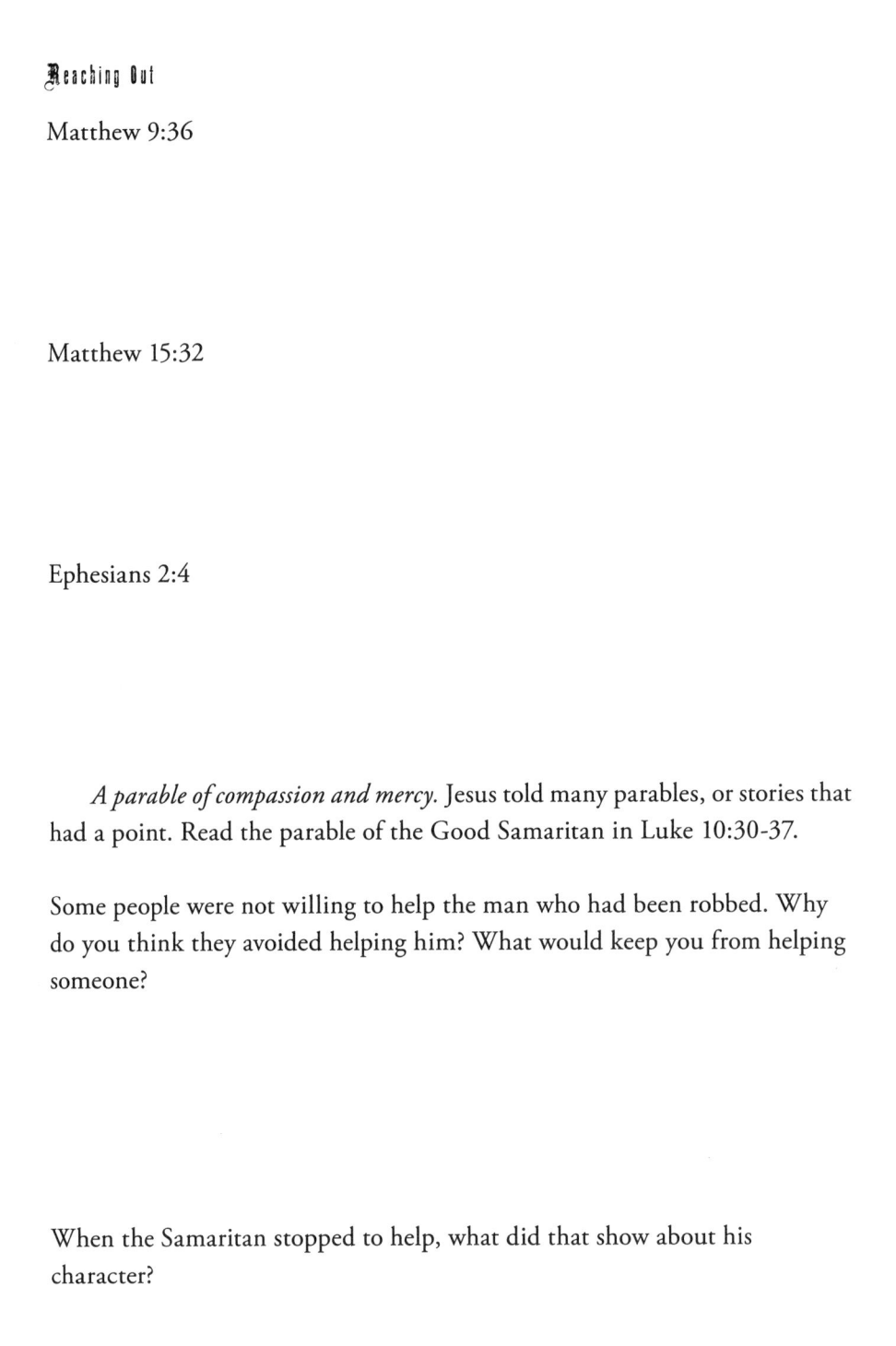

Matthew 9:36

Matthew 15:32

Ephesians 2:4

A parable of compassion and mercy. Jesus told many parables, or stories that had a point. Read the parable of the Good Samaritan in Luke 10:30-37.

Some people were not willing to help the man who had been robbed. Why do you think they avoided helping him? What would keep you from helping someone?

When the Samaritan stopped to help, what did that show about his character?

Why do you think Jesus told this story? What does it mean to you?

A challenge. The Lord is challenging us to be compassionate and merciful. Read these verses and reflect on what you think God is asking you to do.

Psalm 72:12-14

Zechariah 7:9-10

Matthew 5:7

Colossians 3:12

DO THIS AT HOME THIS WEEK

- Was there someone you should have served in the last twenty-four hours? Write down what prevented you from serving that person.
- Identify one problem in your community, school, or church. Consider how your action could bring about change and meet that need. Is there a way for you to get involved?
- Think of one person who has a need that you can meet. Write down one way in which you can show compassion or mercy to that person. Now do it!
- Read "Hope for a Nation" on pages 105-107 of this book. Consider the challenge that closes this story.

PRAYER TIME

- Ask the Lord to help you understand what it means to be a person of compassion and mercy.
- Pray that the Lord will direct you as you seek to show compassion and mercy to those around you.
- Ask God for guidance as you look for ways to take action and be involved in bringing about positive changes.

MEMORY VERSE

Since God chose you to be the holy people he loves, you must clothe yourselves with tenderhearted mercy, kindness, humility, gentleness, and patience. (Colossians 3:12)

Being a Servant Leader (Part 2)

>> And whatever you do or say, do it as a representative of the Lord Jesus, giving thanks through him to God the Father. (Colossians 3:17)

In our last session we began a study of what it means to be a servant leader. This session continues that study.

characteristic 4: hospitality

A servant leader will be a person who shows hospitality to others.

How would you define "hospitality"?

Reaching Out

The Bible gives us many examples of people who showed hospitality. Read these passages and summarize what happened in your own words. What does each of the following examples show us about hospitality?

Genesis 18:1-8

Genesis 24:31-33

1 Kings 17:8-16

2 Kings 4:8-10

How might the Lord challenge you to show hospitality? Is this something you think you're already good at or not? How could you grow in this skill?

Read and reflect on these verses. Write them in your own words.

Romans 12:13

1 Timothy 3:2

Matthew 25:37-40

Hebrews 13:2

Colossians 1:10

Galatians 6:8-10

characteristic 5: humility

A servant leader will be humble.

Write a definition of *humility* in your own words.

Philippians 2:5-11 explains how Jesus demonstrated humility. Read this passage, and then answer the following questions:

Although Jesus is God, in what four ways did He show humility?

How does Jesus' obedience to God, and His dying on the cross, show humility?

When Jesus humbled Himself, what did God the Father do? What does this mean to you?

If people are not confident that the Lord is watching over them and in control, sometimes they may find it difficult to be humble in front of others. Making ourselves look better in the eyes of others is pride. Trusting that Jesus will lift us up in the eyes of others, if He so chooses, results in humility.

Read Luke 14:8-11 and think about what Jesus is saying to you. How does this passage challenge you? What could you change to demonstrate more humility?

Jesus gives us a direct challenge to be humble in Philippians 2:3-4. What is that challenge? How can you respond?

characteristic 6: brokenness

Being "broken" is a way of saying that we recognize that our lives are damaged, and that God can still use us in this state. We may have poor health, have had a difficult life, may be going through financial troubles . . . no matter what the situation, none of us has everything together or has a perfect life. We are broken. A servant leader recognizes this and doesn't try to cover it up. He or she is honest about being in this condition, and allows God to use that brokenness for His glory.

A leader who is broken before the Lord will be more sensitive to the needs of the people he or she is leading and will be more likely to be available for the Lord to use.

Consider Paul. He was challenged to boast of his successes, but he preferred to boast about his failures.

Read 2 Corinthians 11:16–12:10. What did Paul have to boast about? Why do you think he wanted to boast about his failures? How could God use failure to bring glory to Himself?

Paul was given a physical weakness to keep him from getting proud, and he realized that through his weakness and brokenness Jesus could be stronger in him. It's very important for a leader to understand the significance of weakness in God's kingdom. Godly leaders don't do God's work; rather, they let God do His work through them. Brokenness helps this process.

Psalm 51:16-17 tells us that God's greatest delight does not come from our sacrifices or our offerings, but from brokenness and a repentant heart. A broken and repentant heart is a humble heart toward God and the people around us. A broken heart, in this instance, is the heart of a person who recognizes his or her failures and total need for God. It is the heart of a person who sees that apart from Jesus nothing of any real significance can be done (see John 15:5), and he or she is surrendered completely to Christ as Lord. This leader does not place confidence in his or her own abilities, but rather has total confidence in the Lord. Being broken makes the leader sensitive and compassionate.

characteristic 7: thankfulness

A servant leader will have an attitude of gratefulness or thankfulness toward God and others. When a leader communicates gratitude and thanks, that person shows that he or she appreciates and values others.

How do these verses challenge you concerning your attitudes of thankfulness? Summarize your thoughts on each verse.

Psalm 100:4

Psalm 95:2

Ephesians 1:15-16

2 Thessalonians 1:3

Philippians 4:10

1 Corinthians 16:17-18

Luke 17:11-19

Reaching Out

It is clear in the Bible that the Lord wants us to be thankful. The Scriptures also suggest some of the things for which we should be thankful.

Summarize what you notice in the following verses.

Daniel 2:23

John 6:11

John 11:41

1 Corinthians 15:57

1 Thessalonians 1:2

1 Thessalonians 2:13

2 Corinthians 12:9-10

What are you thankful for? How many things can you list in one minute? What are things that you never thought about being thankful for that these verses have suggested to you? Can you be thankful for those things? Why or why not?

DO THIS AT HOME THIS WEEK

- Write down at least 10 things for which you are thankful.
- Make a list of things you feel a bit too proud to willingly do. Be honest. This might include cleaning someone's toilet, changing a diaper, washing dishes, or another unpleasant chore. Pray about this list, asking God to give you a humble heart and a willingness to do anything He asks if it will show love to another person.
- Consider a way to show hospitality to someone this week. What could you do? When will you do it?
- As you consider what it means to be a servant leader who is broken, reflect on these things:
  - Consider where you lack in being faithful. Be honest with yourself.
  - Confess your failure to Jesus and thank Him for His forgiveness and restoration.
  - Confess to a trusted friend or leader your failures in being obedient to Jesus (James 5:16).

Reaching Out

Ask Jesus to give you the strength, through His Spirit, to obey Him moment by moment. Ask your friends to hold you accountable for the promises you made.

PRAYER TIME

- Praise Jesus for who He is. Thank Him for what He is doing in your life.
- Take a few minutes right now to thank the Lord for the things you listed.
- Pray that the Lord will give you the boldness and humility to serve another person, no matter how unpleasant the task may seem.

MEMORY VERSE

So humble yourselves under the mighty power of God, and at the right time he will lift you up in honor. (1 Peter 5:6)

Bonus!

In this section you'll find additional readings, as well as helpful tools for leading a small group using this book.

Be Bold!

Having difficulty getting up the courage to share your faith with others? That's because being different and standing up for something others don't care about can be scary. When we stand out in the crowd we're vulnerable, and it can be intimidating. Boldness can be a very real need.

Read Acts 16:16-24 and 1 Thessalonians 2:1-2.

How do these accounts encourage or discourage you to be bold?

What is at risk when you're bold about your faith?

To be bold is to be courageous, confident, and willing to take action, even in the face of danger. Most of us think of bold people as unafraid, pushing forward, not embarrassed by anything, or very outgoing. You may be picturing an extreme athlete, a military leader, a controversial speaker, or a salesperson who won't take "no" for an answer. We don't think of a quiet grandfather or a shy, thirteen-year-old girl as bold, but they can be!

why be bold about faith?

- It takes boldness to be different from others. Jesus said in Matthew 5:15 that no one lights a lamp and then hides it under a basket. Instead, they put the lamp out where it can shine and show the way around the room. This means that we are to stand out and shine in our good works and actions. This can be very hard.
- It takes boldness to publicly own our relationship with Jesus. Matthew 10:32-33 says, "Everyone who acknowledges me publicly here on earth, I will also acknowledge before my Father in heaven. But everyone who denies me here on earth, I will also deny before my Father in heaven." It's a serious matter to deny the Lord before others, so at times we are called to be bold.
- We need to be bold and confident (but not arrogant) so that people around us will know that we serve a God who is alive and at work in us. If we become timid and embarrassed, the message we send may be that our God is not big enough to help us.
- With Jesus' boldness in us we can be confident because Jesus is the Truth. The Bible says in Proverbs 28:1, "The wicked run away when no one is chasing them, but the godly are as bold as lions." We may be afraid of sharing our faith because we feel we're not good enough. We become afraid of people, rejection, ridicule, failure, and so on. At these times we need to remember that Jesus is bold within us. He gives us the strength to stand.
- We need boldness because people are important to God. We are so loved by God and so precious to Him, that Jesus gave His life for all of us. We can be bold as we offer hope to all those whom God loves.

How do we become more bold?
It's easy to *talk* about being more bold . . . but in reality, it can be hard!

We find ourselves weak—afraid of sharing our faith, afraid of being made fun of, afraid that we might make mistakes, and afraid that the person we're sharing with might reject us and Jesus. So the issue is, how do we trust Jesus in our weakness?

We can look at examples of great bravery and courage, where followers of Jesus were prepared even to die for their faith in Jesus. You'll find many of these in the Bible, and there are many books about more recent Christians who have given everything for their faith in Jesus. Here are a few from the Bible you can read about:

Read Acts 7:51-60 and 2 Corinthians 11:16-33.

These people prayed for courage. God heard their prayers directly and they were able to speak the Word of God with boldness. It was the Spirit of God in them that gave them strength. So when we feel inadequate, we can pray for God to give us His boldness, and He will respond. This doesn't mean that we won't be rejected, we won't be made fun of, or even that we won't be harmed. But it does mean that God will give us boldness.

> Alexander the Great had a soldier in his army who bore his own name, but the man was a great coward. The Emperor, enraged at this man's conduct, justly said to him, "Either change your name, or learn to honor it." *What does this mean to you as a Christian, who carries the name of Jesus Christ?*

are you bold for Jesus?

As followers of Jesus, we are called to be "on fire" for Christ. Not warm, but burning. In fact, if we are just "lukewarm," Jesus says in Revelations 3:16 that He will spit us out of His mouth! It's easy to be comfortable and safe, but we are called to be followers who are excited about our friendship with Jesus and ready to share about it.

Are you constantly growing in your ability to show grace and love to others? How do you see yourself growing in this area?

Reaching Out

Do you openly share about your faith to friends and family on a daily basis, or do you rarely speak of Him?

Are you passionate about knowing Jesus in a deeper way and sharing what you're discovering?

Every day brings us a new challenge to follow Christ. We may fail at times. However, as we grow in our relationship with Christ, we can learn from our failures and become stronger and bolder for Jesus. Think about these situations you might face. How can you be bold?

Your friends are making fun of someone. Will you quietly laugh along, or will you boldly stand up for the victim of their cruelty? What do you think will happen?

In a conversation with friends, the topic of religious beliefs is brought up by someone. Will you shy away from sharing about your love for Jesus? Or will you boldly speak of what He's done for you — and for them, too?

You're at a movie with friends, and the content is clearly not honoring Christ. Will you sit quietly and watch or take a risk and leave? Or will you talk to your friends about what's offensive to you in this movie?

List three other situations you might face in your normal, day-to-day life where you can be bold about Jesus.

Share a time when you were not bold for Christ. What could you have done differently now that you've had time to think about it?

Share about a time when you were bold for Christ, even though you might have been afraid.

Think of actions — not words — you can use to share your love for Christ with others.

What it Means to Believe in Jesus

> Then God said, "Let us make human beings in our image, to be like us. They will reign over the fish in the sea, the birds in the sky, the livestock, all the wild animals on the earth, and the small animals that scurry along the ground."
>
> So God created human beings in his own image. In the image of God he created them; male and female he created them.
>
> Then God blessed them and said, "Be fruitful and multiply. Fill the earth and govern it. Reign over the fish in the sea, the birds in the sky, and all the animals that scurry along the ground."
>
> Then God said, "Look! I have given you every seed-bearing plant throughout the earth and all the fruit trees for your food. And I have given every green plant as food for all the wild animals, the birds in the sky, and the small animals that scurry along the ground—everything that has life." And that is what happened. Then God looked over all he had made, and he saw that it was very good!
>
> And evening passed and morning came, marking the sixth day. (Genesis 1:26-31)

The Bible tells us that at the very beginning God created us in His image and gave us command over the rest of His creation. When God looked at all that He had made, He was very pleased. Unfortunately, God's ideal creation was ruined by rebellion when Adam and Eve ate from the forbidden tree, disobeying God (Genesis 3). The result of their disobedience was a break in the relationship between people and God. This was the beginning of the evil desires and actions of us all, which results in our death and eternal separation from God.

In order to bring God and us together, God, in His love, sent His Son Jesus to save us, and give us another chance for life — this time forever, but only if we believe.

During His lifetime, Jesus Christ met many different needs of the people around Him. He healed the sick, cast out demons, raised the dead, and fed thousands of hungry people. However, His ultimate reason for coming to earth was not just to heal our bodies, but to heal our hearts with His love. Not just to raise the dead, but to keep us alive in Him forever. Not just to feed thousands of hungry people, but to fill any hungry heart yearning for His love. He would have come even if there was only one hungry heart left on earth.

The Bible says in Romans 10:13, "Everyone who calls on the name of the Lord will be saved." So if you have asked Him into your life and believe He died to save you, you have become a follower of Jesus. You are now a new creation! This is the incredible message that you are being encouraged to share throughout this book.

Evangelism Is Important

Evangelism is so important . . .

. . . because we and all people and all of creation were made to shout out God's glory. Did you see the sun radiate His glory this morning? Or hear the birds sing? Psalm 148 says it all. We want to help the world praise its maker and rejoice in what we all have been given.

Evangelism is so important . . .

. . . because God's love for His people is so great He sent His son Jesus to be humbled and become a man and die on a cross in order that we might live and have an eternal relationship with Him. His love for us is our best example for loving others. John 15:13 says, "There is no greater love than to lay down one's life for one's friends." What an amazing example!

Evangelism is so important .

. . . because of our love for our family, friends, and wider communities. How can we *not* share the love we have within us to those who struggle and have little hope in themselves or their world?

Evangelism is so important . . .

. . . because the gospel message is so valuable. Jesus described it as a pearl of great price or a hidden treasure a person would sell everything to get. Nothing in life has greater value than this. The angels' announcement about Jesus' birth was, "I bring you good news that will bring great joy to all people. The Savior—yes, the Messiah, the Lord—has been born today in Bethlehem, the city of David!" (Luke 2:10-11).

Evangelism is so important . . .

. . . because the gift is free and for everyone. A simple act of faith is all that's necessary to experience God's grace and forgiveness. Ephesians 2:8-9 tells us, "God saved you by his grace when you believed. And you can't take credit for this; it is a gift from God. Salvation is not a reward for the good things we have done, so none of us can boast about it."

Can you think of any other reasons why evangelism is important? If so, write them here.

Go and Do the Same

Servant leadership means taking an active part in our schools, communities, churches, and nation with a view of encouraging positive and godly change in the lives of others. It also means living as a Christian in our society—being a practical example of Christian love will bring joy and gladness to the lives of people who are hurting and suffering. We also long to bring about reconciliation between divided and fighting people groups, whether the division is based on religious, ethnic, economic, or other differences.

We are Christ in action—being the salt of the earth; a light to our generation. It is our worship, our service with and in Christ as we stand up for what is truth and right.

In Luke 10, Jesus told the following story after a man asked, "Who is my neighbor?"

> A Jewish man was traveling on a trip from Jerusalem to Jericho, and he was attacked by bandits. They stripped him of his clothes, beat him up, and left him half dead beside the road.
>
> By chance a priest came along. But when he saw the man lying there, he crossed to the other side of the road and passed him by. A Temple assistant walked over and looked at him lying there, but he also passed by on the other side.

Then a despised Samaritan came along, and when he saw the man, he felt compassion for him. Going over to him, the Samaritan soothed his wounds with olive oil and wine and bandaged them. Then he put the man on his own donkey and took him to an inn, where he took care of him. The next day he handed the innkeeper two silver coins, telling him, "Take care of this man. If his bill runs higher than this, I'll pay you the next time I'm here."

"Now which of these three would you say was a neighbor to the man who was attacked by bandits?" Jesus asked.

The man replied, "The one who showed him mercy."

Then Jesus said, "Yes, now go and do the same." (Luke 10:30-37)

In this parable, Jesus taught a powerful lesson about our responsibility to show practical love. The Good Samaritan is an excellent model, challenging us to love through service and sacrifice.

Jesus said, "Go and do the same." What does that mean to you?

Hope for a Nation

In 1994 one million people were murdered in just one hundred days—most of them brutally killed with machetes. The ruthlessness and extent of this genocide is impossible to comprehend and can only really be understood by those who lived through it. How could so many be killed in such a vicious way and in such a short period of time?

This horrific genocide was achieved by mobilizing the youth of Rwanda; teenagers and young adults carried out the slaughter. Satan knows that if you empower young people and harness all of their energy, creativity, innocence, and unswerving commitment to a cause, you can achieve almost anything, either for good or for evil.

Satan used the youth of Rwanda to ravage, murder, and destroy, but God is using the young people of this nation to rebuild and to bring about enormous change for good. In the past ten years, through the support of ministry partners like you, 350,000 young people have been reached and 70,000 of these have committed their lives to Christ. By the end of 2005, 800 young leaders were trained, and through them 100,000 more young people were reached. Rwanda is now a nation being rebuilt by young people who are "sold out" to Jesus. In the face of unbelievable suffering, evil, and destruction, these young people are living out their faith through love, grace, forgiveness, purity, self-sacrifice, and servanthood.

Reaching Out

Luke is one of these young people. He came to know Christ in 1995, just one year after the genocide. Soon after committing himself to Jesus, Luke attended Youth for Christ's Rwanda Leadership and Discipleship training program. Through this program, God began to prepare Luke for leadership.

Luke returned to his local church, which had no pastor or leader. Even though he was only 18 years old, Luke became the church leader. He began a sports program as a local outreach to young people, using basketball, soccer, and volleyball as a means of beginning a friendship with them.

When the schools reopened in Rwanda, Luke started YFC Bible clubs at his local school. He also organized YFC Bible Clubs in other local high schools, expanding the ministry to reach as many people as he could.

Hungry to receive training and grow in his relationship with God, Luke attended every YFC Youth Leadership Training program that was offered. During school holidays, he and other young YFC leaders would attend Bible studies in the home of YFC Rwanda's National Director, Jean-Baptiste. Soon Luke and another young leader, Johanna, became prayer partners. They prayed together early each Tuesday morning before school.

After finishing school, Luke began a career in business and then went to work for a local non-government organization, earning a great deal of money. Luke began to notice corruption there and eventually decided that he could no longer commit to this organization. He continued working in business, but Luke's passion for reaching young people led him to volunteer for YFC coordinating and training.

In 2002, Luke followed God's leading and joined Youth for Christ full-time, becoming the Coordinator for Volunteers and expanding his role to coordinate volunteers for the whole nation. There are now more than 400 volunteers and twelve paid staff under his leadership.

Through Luke's leadership, 100,000 people were reached in 2005. Through training young people and organizing them in teams that are sent throughout Rwanda, more and more people are reached with the love of Jesus.

Recently, teams under Luke's leadership went to three areas in southern Rwanda. At least 15,000 people came to listen to the gospel, with about 3,000 of them receiving Jesus Christ into their lives. In one area, pastors couldn't believe what they saw as teams ministered on the streets and in marketplaces. The boldness of the YFC staff and volunteers overwhelmed everyone who witnessed it.

Rwanda is now a nation being rebuilt by young people like Luke who are committed to Jesus.

This story shows the impact of what just one person did. What does Luke's example inspire you to do?

How do you envision teenagers and young adults making a difference for God in your community in the coming months and years?

Small Group Leader's Guide

How to Lead a Small Group

If you're using this book with a small group, you'll find it's easy to follow along. Simply read sections in each session aloud together, and when you're instructed to write your reflections, take additional time to discuss these in your group instead of just writing those thoughts.

You'll also find additional ideas for each session later in this section. These are optional ideas, but they'll help get your group thinking about the topic at hand. Give them a try!

Here are a few more tips that will make your group a success.

- Be sure your small groups really are small. If you have more than six people in your group, form smaller groups. By keeping groups at six or fewer members, you allow everyone time to talk, and people will generally open up and be more honest when sharing in a very small group.
- Take your time and work through each session, allowing time for Scripture reading, discussion, and prayer. Allow at least an hour for each session. You may want to allow more time so no one feels rushed during discussion.
- When there are lists of passages to look up and comment on, assign different small groups the different passages. Allow them several

minutes to look up and read their passage, and discuss it together. Then have each group report back to the larger group about what they read, what they learned, and what their action steps might be.

- Ask each person to also do the "Do This at Home This Week" section during the week before you meet again. It's a great idea to have at least ten minutes at the beginning of each meeting to hear reports back on how people did with these challenges. Celebrate the growth you see in each other's lives as you hear what's happened since you last met.
- Don't let any one person monopolize the discussions. Encourage everyone to share, and monitor the discussion by drawing out the quieter people with questions such as, "We haven't heard from Aiko yet. Let's hear your opinion, Aiko." Or you could say, "We've heard a lot from Joaquin on this question, but I want to be sure everyone has a chance to share. Tony, what are your thoughts?" Be gentle, but do let it be known that everyone is equal in the discussion.
- Remind group members that what is shared with the group is confidential. No one wants to be the subject of gossip.
- Everyone in your group will need a Bible and pen, along with a copy of this book. Encourage responsibility by asking everyone to remember to bring these.
- Start on time and end on time. It honors the commitment of those who are attending.
- Provide snacks. This is optional, but you'll find everyone will appreciate it!

Group Discussion Starters

In this section you'll find optional activities to use with your small group. These can be used to begin each of your sessions as a way to engage your group and prepare them for further reflection and discussion.

SESSION ONE: REASONS TO SHARE
Here's a simple way to get everyone ready to consider why we share our faith in Jesus. Have everyone find a partner and answer this question: How can you tell if someone loves you?

After several minutes of discussion, have everyone find a new partner and answer this question: What's the coolest thing anyone has ever done to show you his or her love?

After several minutes of discussion, have everyone return to the larger group and allow several people to share what was discussed with their partners. Then continue with the session.

SESSION TWO: GOD'S STORY AND MY STORY
This game is a fun way to get everyone thinking about what makes a good story. You'll need sheets of paper.

Give each person a sheet of paper. Explain that at the top of the page each person should write the first sentence of a story. It can be one they've made up, a line from a fable or story they know from childhood, or even the start of a plot of a movie they've seen. Allow one minute, and then have each person fold the part they wrote down so no one can see that sentence. Have each person pass his or her paper to the right.

Reaching Out

Ask people to continue the story they started on the first piece of paper—although obviously now they're writing it on someone else's story. Have everyone write the second sentence to his or her story, then fold this down, and again pass the paper to the right. Continue this until each paper has been passed about five times. Have the person holding each paper write a final sentence and "The end."

Now take turns reading these stories aloud. You're sure to have a few laughs at what was created, and it will be funny to see how all these stories mixed together make something new. Some stories will be nonsense, while others might actually be amusing new tales.

Use this to then lead into the concept of sharing our stories with others, and that we all love a good story—even a silly one that makes us laugh!

Note: Prepare for the next session by having each person bring a book that they loved to read as a child. These will be used in the optional opening for session three.

SESSION THREE: MY STORY AND YOUR STORY

As the idea of using our stories to share our faith is continued in this session, you'll use an activity that reminds everyone of those favorite stories from childhood. Hopefully you asked each person to bring a book that he or she enjoyed as a child. Even if people didn't bring their books, this activity will still work.

Remind group members that they were to bring a favorite childhood book for this session. For those who forgot to bring a book, they can think about what their favorite book was and share about it.

Go around the circle and have each person show (or at least tell the name of) his or her favorite book or story from childhood. Ask them to share why this story was such a special one at that time of life, and if they still enjoy reading it today. You can take this discussion a bit deeper by asking if there were lessons learned from this story that can be applied to life today.

Use this sharing activity to again help everyone understand the importance of sharing their own stories with others, and getting to know the stories of those they hope to tell about Jesus. A good story can be powerful and hard to forget—and often continues to leave an impression in our minds years later.

For added impact, have each person put away the book they brought, and then go around the circle and see if everyone can remember what title others shared about. After all, this session does focus on good listening skills. How well did everyone do?

SESSION FOUR: GOD'S STORY AND YOUR STORY

This session finishes the discussion on using story to share our faith, and in one section encourages group members to find ways of using real-life situations as examples of what God is doing in our lives. This activity stretches group members to find ways to use other popular activities as they share their faith.

Have group members form pairs, and ask each pair to decide on a book, movie, or song that they both are familiar with and write that title down. After each pair has decided, read this scenario and have them discuss these questions:

> Imagine that you have another friend who doesn't know Jesus. This friend also likes the book, movie, or song that you've written down. How could you use the message of your chosen title to start a conversation about God? What would be a non-judgmental and non-threatening way to use the message of this book, movie, or song to engage your friend in a discussion about God?

Allow about five minutes for pairs to discuss their thoughts on this, and then have a few of them report back to the larger group. Use this as a springboard for the session.

SESSION FIVE: FRIENDSHIP EVANGELISM

This activity reminds us of the great news we have to share, and that we've got every reason to spread that message to our friends.

Have each person think of the best news they've heard or experienced that day, but not say it out loud. This might be a good grade on a test, news that a family member is recovering from a long illness, getting a new dog, or anything else that might be considered good news.

When everyone has a "good news" story in mind, explain that everyone has two minutes to tell as many people in the room about this message as possible. Group members should try to keep track of how many people they tell as they're quickly spreading the good news around the room. Start timing, and say, "Go!" After two minutes, call time. Have everyone tell how many people they were able to share their good news with. Then have group members discuss how hard or easy it was to share this news. What made it hard? What made it easy?

Use this discussion to segue into the topic of sharing the good news of Jesus with friends through friendship evangelism.

SESSION SIX: PRAYER EVANGELISM

This is a simple way to get everyone thinking about how many opportunities they have for prayer in a day.

Have everyone go outside for five minutes with this instruction: Try to remember as many things as you can that you see in five minutes. You can't write anything down—you'll have to rely on your memory.

Send everyone outside, and after five minutes gather group members inside again. Give each person a pen and paper and have them write as many things as they can remember. See who has the longest list (perhaps reward that person with an extra cookie or other treat).

Then ask members to look at those lists. Can they think of something to pray about that is associated with each item on that list? For example, a leaf might be a reason to thank God for His creation, school could remind someone to pray for a friend who goes there or the teachers there, a car could remind a group member to pray for safety for those traveling, and so on.

Then move into the session and how important prayer is in leading someone into a relationship with Jesus. Encourage group members to use these lists, or make new ones, as reminders to always be in prayer.

SESSION SEVEN: PRAYER GROUPS

As this session focuses on the power of praying in a group, this active game will get everyone thinking about the strength found in numbers. You'll need scraps of paper.

Have everyone find a partner. Have each pair crumple up one piece of paper to make a small ball. Explain that partners will play "catch" with the paper ball, tossing it back and forth and catching it, with this one small rule: They must make a fist, extend only their index finger on that hand, and only use that one finger to toss and catch the ball. This won't be too hard when they're throwing the ball . . . but catching it is a different matter!

After a minute or two of flying paper balls, stop everyone and explain that now they can use all the fingers on that hand instead of being limited to one. Play for another minute or two, then have the group return to their seats. Discuss these questions:

- What could you do with five fingers that you couldn't do with just one?
- What are other examples of the saying "There's strength in numbers" being true?

Group Discussion Starters

Use this to segue into the topic of praying in groups, and the strength that comes from being united in prayer with others.

SESSION EIGHT: POWER EVANGELISM

As this session focuses on the power of God's Holy Spirit, use this opening activity to get everyone thinking about the importance of unseen power in their own lives. You'll need a variety of battery-operated items, such as toys, flashlights, or tools. Take the batteries out of these and set them aside.

Distribute the items you've brought and let everyone try to use them. Some may be used without the batteries, but without much effect (such as a stuffed animal that is still cuddly but doesn't bark or walk around the room as it could). Others, such as a flashlight, will be useless without a power source.

After allowing a few minutes for experimenting, distribute the batteries and let everyone use the items as they are intended for a few minutes. Then put these items away and discuss the difference in each item when it had a power source. What was the difference? What are other items we use every day that require a power source, even if we don't see that source with our eyes (such as the wind, or electricity that we only see as a power outlet on the wall)?

Use this conversation to move into a discussion of God's power in evangelism and how, even though we cannot see God's power with our eyes, we can see its effect and the difference it makes.

SESSION NINE: WHO WE ARE IN GOD'S EYES

This session uses a story by an unknown author to demonstrate the value of each person. Take the story a bit further by using this as an opening illustration. You'll need money bills of a low denomination (or if you're willing to spend more, use money worth more). Try to find the newest and crispest money possible.

Gather your group together and show them the money. Ask if anyone wants it, because you're willing to give it away. Certainly a few hands will be raised. Then crumple the money. See if anyone still wants it. Stand on it, rub dirt on it, tear off a small corner, maybe even tear it in half then tape it back together. After each of these, ask if anyone still wants the money. Finally give it to someone in the group — perhaps the person wearing the most blue — and ask how that person will use the money.

Ask everyone why they were willing to take the money no matter what shape it was in. Then compare this to our value to God. Why is God willing to take us no matter what shape we're in? Why does money have value no matter

Reaching Out

what? Why do we have value no matter what?

Use this to move into the session on why we are of such incredible value to God.

SESSION TEN: MEETING THE NEEDS OF OTHERS

This game gets everyone thinking about how simple it can be to meet a need . . . and how funny it is when the need is met with the wrong action. You'll need index cards.

Give each person two index cards. Explain that each person is to write a problem on one card and a simple solution for that problem on the other card. For example, a group member might write, "I have a headache" on one card, and "Take an aspirin" on the other card. Or someone might write, "My clothes are dirty" on one card, and then "I'll do the laundry" on the other card.

After everyone has written on both cards, collect the cards, keeping the problem cards in one stack and the solution cards in another stack. Then redistribute the cards so everyone gets a new problem card and a random solution card. Go around the group, having each person read their problem card first ("I have a headache") and the new solution that they're going to try ("I'll do the laundry"). These will surely get everyone laughing.

Use this to move into the topic of how simple it really can be to meet needs of others, as long as we're listening to their real needs and looking for a practical solution!

SESSION ELEVEN: BEING A SERVANT LEADER (PART 1)

As you move into the two sessions on what it means to be a servant leader, this activity will get everyone thinking about how radical this idea truly is.

Form groups of three or four. Explain that each group has five minutes to create an advertisement for a new leader, and they need to be sure to mention five qualities that make their leader the best.

Have fun with this! It could be a new political leader, new group leader, leader of a new club—any kind of leader. The leader that they're making the advertisement for could be a real person (it could be one of the group members!) or it could be a fictional person they've invented. Just be sure that five qualities about that person are mentioned.

Allow five minutes for groups to work together and plan their advertisement; then it's show time! Once all the advertisements have been presented, see if everyone can remember the qualities that were used to describe these potential new leaders. Was servanthood or being a servant mentioned even once?

Discuss what qualities everyone thinks makes a good leader, and then move into this session and the concept of being a servant leader.

SESSION TWELVE: BEING A SERVANT LEADER (PART 2)

Think about this. Mother Teresa became an influential leader—on the world level—by being a servant. Using one of her most famous quotes will spark discussion as your group continues to explore what it means to be a servant leader.

Read this quote from Mother Teresa: "We can do no great things, only small things with great love." Discuss:

- What does this mean?
- Do you think this statement is true or not? Explain.
- If this quote is true, how would it change your perspective on leadership?

After a time of discussion, move into the final session on being a servant leader.

Youth for Christ

Youth for Christ is a global indigenous Christian youth movement active in one hundred nations worldwide.

YFC programs are led by a national director and board made up of nationals from each country. In this way, YFC is able to reach young people around the world in a context that makes sense to them and their culture.

YFC has successfully reached young people with the gospel of Christ since the 1940s. From its then first employee, Billy Graham, to the now 35,000 international staff and volunteers, YFC continues to minister to young people worldwide.

God is calling Youth for Christ to invest in reaching and engaging young people for Jesus Christ, equipping them as His disciples and empowering them as godly leaders to transform the world.

YFC's strategic focus is to reach young people everywhere, working together with the local church and other like-minded partners to raise up lifelong followers of Jesus who lead by their godliness in lifestyle, devotion to the Word of God and prayer, passion for sharing the love of Christ and commitment to social involvement.

Also Available in the YOUTH FOR CHRIST JOURNEY Series!

Youth for Christ presents the JOURNEY series, a four-part Bible study that looks closely at the basic concepts of leadership, sharing your faith, God's kingdom, and spiritual warfare. In each study, you'll find an easy-to-read format with stories from around the world, Scripture, and lots of space to write down your thoughts.

Faith Journey
ISBN-13: 978-1-60006-314-5
ISBN-10: 1-60006-314-4

Have you put off becoming a follower of Christ? Maybe you don't see the importance or you have too many questions to make the decision. This study helps you answer your questions and learn about the Savior who calls to you. A life of completeness, wholeness, and peace awaits.

Influencing Others
ISBN-13: 978-1-60006-315-2
ISBN-10: 1-60006-315-2

Leadership isn't just about power, authority, fame, or money; it's about influencing others and making things happen. Along with learning the characteristics of leaders and how to influence people in a godly way, you'll discover the importance of serving the ones who follow you and serving Christ as you lead.

Spiritual Warfare
ISBN-13: 978-1-60006-316-9
ISBN-10: 1-60006-316-0

Are you confused about spiritual warfare and what it involves? You're not alone. Lots of people are in the dark about battling the powers of darkness. Learn what spiritual warfare is and how praise, prayer, and authority are used. Battle the darkness with the power of God.

To order copies, call NavPress at
1-800-366-7788 or log on to www.navpress.com.

NAVPRESS®